Black Heroes

IN MONOLOGUES

D1490298

Black Heroes

IN MONOLOGUES

Gus Edwards

HEINEMANN
PORTSMOUTH, NH

Heinemann

812.54
Edw

A division of Reed Elsevier Inc.
361 Hanover Street
Portsmouth, NH 03801–3912
www.heinemanndrama.com

Offices and agents throughout the world

Performance rights information can be found on p. 146.

CIP data is on file at the Library of Congress.
ISBN: 0-325-00925-2

Editor: Lisa A. Barnett
Production: Vicki Kasabian
Cover design: Catherine Hawkes, Cat & Mouse Design
Cover photo: ©iStockphoto.com/Diane Diederich
Typesetter: Tom Allen, Pear Graphic Design
Manufacturing: Steve Bernier

Printed in the United States of America on acid-free paper
10 09 08 07 06   VP   1 2 3 4 5

CONTENTS

Introduction vii

Alberta Hunter 1
 "Why I Sung the Blues" 1

August Wilson 4
 "Just Chattin'" 5

Bass Reeves 8
 "Knowing the Territory" 9

Booker T. Washington 13
 "The Final Key" 13

Charles "Buddy" Bolden 17
 "My Own Private Blues" 17
 "Witness to the Starting" (*remembering
 Buddy Bolden*) 21

Coretta Scott King 31
 "I Remember" 31

Elizabeth Hudson Smith 34
 "A Monument to Me" 35

Frederick Douglass 41
 "Talkin' 'Bout Slavery" (*a rap*) 41
 "I Will Raise Both My Hands" 46

"General" Buddoe 50
 "We Will Ask, But We Won't Beg" 50

Harriet Tubman 54
 "Mr. John Brown and Me" 54

Hattie McDaniel 59
 "Nobody Knows and Yet They Talk" 59

Jackie Robinson 65
 "Baseball and Character" 65

James Baldwin   69
    "A Dream of Deliverance" (*a dual monologue*)   69

Joe Louis   74
    "Faithful to the End"   74

Joseph Cinque   80
    "Memories of the *Amistad*"   80

Daniel Louis "Satch" Armstrong   88
    "Riffing"   89

Mahalia Jackson   92
    "The Honest-to-God Truth" (*young Mahalia*)   92
    "Why I Sing Gospel"   98

Malcolm X   101
    "Changes"   102

Dr. Martin Luther King Jr.   105
    "I Want to Make This Clear"   105

Nat Turner   109
    "Meditations" (*on the eve of his
    bold and daring enterprise*)   109

Oscar Micheaux   115
    "Ambition and Optimism"   115

Paul Robeson   121
    "Who I Am, What I Stand For"   122

"Queen" Mary   125
    "Tired a Waitin'"   125

Ralph Johnson Bunche   128
    "A New World Order" (*a prayer*)   128

Rosa Parks   132
    "Unsung Heroes"   132

St. Martin de Porres   137
    "I Am Blessed"   137

Sojourner Truth   141
    "The Power of Words: Starting to Learn"   141

Performance Rights   146

INTRODUCTION

About six years ago, I was a guest lecturer at a university not my own, talking about the state of black theatre and other related topics. Over lunch, one of the instructors I had met, an African American woman, drew me off to the side and said she wanted to ask me something. After I told her to go ahead, she said, "Who is Nat Turner, and why is he important?" The reason for the question, she explained, was that his name had been brought up in a class she was teaching, and she had no idea who he was. I told her what I knew about Nat Turner; she thanked me and left.

Several months later, I was talking to a class about my career in theatre and the media work I had done. I mentioned that I had adapted James Baldwin's novel *Go Tell It on the Mountain* as a TV movie and went on to talk about his other books. Something about the expression on the faces of the students told me that they didn't have a clue whom I was talking about. So I asked for a show of hands: who knew about James Baldwin? This was a class of forty-four—three people raised their hand. I pointed to a young African American man and said, "Tell us." He hesitated and said, "I'm not sure, but isn't he related to the Baldwin brothers?" I smiled and gently told him no. I then explained who James Baldwin was and why he is important.

These two incidents became the genesis of this book. I decided I would try to create something that would illuminate the lives and achievements of some African American heroes in a form that was hopefully lively and informative but not at all scholarly (a word which to most students is synonymous with dull). And since I'm a dramatist, not an historian, the idea of monologues came quickly to mind. I would write as if these people were talking to a friend, speaking at a public gathering, or sometimes addressing their Maker in the form of a prayer. This meant I had to read a lot of books, check a lot of facts, and then try as best as I could to channel the mental wavelength of each person, so that I could speak in his or her voice. It was an interesting undertaking, although it led to a certain amount of schizophrenia.

One of the first questions that came up was: *what is a hero—how is one defined?* I went to the dictionary for my answer, and this is what I found. A hero is:

- One who is much admired or shows great courage.
- A person noted for feats of courage and nobility.
- Someone noted for special achievements within a particular field of endeavor.
- The principle character in a literary work.
- In mythology and legend, someone celebrated for his or her bold exploits.

Disregarding the last two definitions, which strictly relate to fictional literary creations, everyone in this book meets the standards of the first three. Still, I had to come up with my own definition of what constitutes a hero. After thinking about it for a while, I came to the conclusion that a hero to me was someone who through some selfless act or deed made the world a better place in one way or another. Loosely following those guidelines, I selected the people in this book. The selections are completely personal. Someone else might've selected a whole host of other individuals as heroes.

That said, I want to emphasize that all the monologues are works of fiction made up by me. They are things I envision this person might have said, not things they actually said. Even in the case of Jackie Robinson, August Wilson, and Louis Armstrong, for whom I tried to reproduce fragments of conversations we had together, there is nothing authentic or accurate about them. They are remembrances from a very faulty memory. Mine.

I wrote this book to acquaint people with some African American heroes they may not have known about, like Bass Reeves or General Buddoe, and some whom they know very well, like Harriet Tubman or Martin Luther King. The monologues are various lengths according to what these persons had to say for themselves. However, Elizabeth Hudson Smith and Buddy Bolden are so little known that I wanted to give them more time on stage in order to provide a fuller picture of who they were, what they did, and the times in which they lived.

These are monologues: they are meant to be read aloud, even acted. I also mean for the reader to have fun with them while learning about some interesting and courageous people. I have tried to be as historically accurate as possible. There is a bit of dramatic license taken now and then, but not much. Otherwise, it would defeat the purpose of this exercise.

Someone once said that black history is either "lost, stolen, or strayed," and to a great extent that is quite true. But a lot of it can be found, not just in musty drawers containing archival material but on the shelves of libraries all over the country. The problem is that not many people go to these books or even know they exist. So the nuances or documented facts of our lives and the lives of our extraordinary citizens go unrecognized and unheralded. This book is in some small measure an attempt to correct this blind spot in our culture.

Black Heroes

IN MONOLOGUES

ALBERTA HUNTER
(1895–1984)

At age twelve Alberta ran away from home in Tennessee and went to Chicago to become a blues singer. After some years of struggle she became one of the most popular singers of the 1920s. Alberta wrote many of the songs she sang, and her "Downhearted Blues" was the first song Bessie Smith recorded in her legendary career. In 1923 Alberta became the first black singer to be backed by a white band. She made many recordings, did a bit of acting, and traveled to Europe, where she was a big hit in Paris. Later on she returned to the United States to take care of her sick mother. When her mother died, in 1956, she gave up singing and worked as a nurse at a hospital in New York City. In 1977, at age eighty-two, she retired from nursing and went back to singing. Her second career was a big success. Her club and concert performances sold out in America and abroad. She was invited to the White House, wrote the score of a movie, and was generally regarded as a living legend. She continued to perform until the day she died.

🔳 Why I Sung the Blues 🔳

Alberta (on an empty stage):

People ask me why I sung the blues . . . well, the blues is to me what milk is to a baby. What the spirit is to a minister. And what good medicine is to a person who's sick. And I should know, because I used to be a nurse. I used to be the one to help them when they was sick in body and mind. But that was a while ago. I's back to singing to cure my soul and the souls of them that listens to me.

Now people always think the blues is sad. They hear people moaning about love that was lost and won't it ever come back again. And sex that was sweet but ain't sweet no more. But that's just one part of the blues. That's just somebody singing slow. Blues is also about joy and happiness and getting revenge. It's about falling in love too. The blues is about telling the truth. Truth telling, I calls it. And that's what I'm doing when I'm singing the blues. I'm truth telling about life.

And everybody want to know why I sing the blues.

I sing the blues because I feel it in my heart and I feel it in my body and in my mind.

"Oh, I hate to see that evening sun go down."

"And man, oh man, if Beale Street could talk it would tell a tale for Shakespeare to hear about fools in love and the wonderment of life."

"St. Louis Blues" is a sad song. The woman in it knows that her man is gone and she's feeling bitter about it. But those feelings pass when you sing them out for everybody to hear. And I should know because I had them all: "The Downhearted Blues." "The Bad Luck Blues." "The Moonshine Blues." "The Lovesick Blues." "Bad Weather Blues." "The Lying and Cheating Blues." "Hard Woman Blues." "Moaning Low Blues." "Sweet Loving Blues." "The Down 'n Dirty Blues." "The Saxophone Blues." "The Shanty Town Blues." Oh, yes, brothers and sisters, I've had them all.

And they knocked me down one or two times. I ain't going to lie to you. They knocked me down good. But with the spirit of the Lord and the power in my soul I got up again. And I'm still standing. Standing on my own two feet. Ain't no man worth it. Or no woman either. And whenever one man goes away, another will come to fill his place.

Ma Rainey, that mean old sister, sang them. Billie Holliday, that sad, lost soul, lived them. Bessie Smith showed the world her behind and then upped and died in that terrible, terrible accident.

At one time or another everybody sings the blues. But me, I try to sing them out every day. Even when I gave up singing I used to sing them to myself just to cleanse out my soul.

And everybody want to know why I sing the blues.

I sing because they pay me money to sing it loud and clear. But the joke of it all is that I would sing even if they didn't pay. But don't tell them that. That's a little secret between you and me.

"I sing the blues," I told that interviewer the other day, "because it's black folks' music. Up from the cotton fields and down into their hearts. We sing the blues because our histories have been hurt and our souls have been disturbed." And I don't know any better reason to give you for singing the blues. And I intend to do it until the day I die.

AUGUST WILSON
(1945–2005)

August Wilson is considered to be among the greatest playwrights America has produced thus far. He was born Frederick August Kittel but used his mother's maiden name, Wilson, when he became a writer. As a young man he worked at menial jobs while submitting poems to black literary magazines. Some were published. Then around 1968 he began writing plays. Most were adaptations of some of his poems. During that time, with a few friends, he even started a small theatre called Black Horizons. But it wasn't until 1983, when his play *Ma Rainey's Black Bottom* was accepted by the Eugene O'Neill Center's National Playwrights Conference, that he began his theatrical career in earnest. There he met Lloyd Richards, artistic director for the conference and dean of the Yale School of Drama, who became his mentor and the director of the first several plays in his ten-play cycle illuminating the African American experience in the United States during all the decades of the twentieth century. *Ma Rainey* and the plays that followed were produced in all the major theatres of America and on Broadway. Wilson quickly became the most honored American playwright of the latter twentieth century, winning many Tony Awards and two Pulitzer Prizes. His ten-play cycle is an unprecedented achievement in American drama. He died of cancer on October 3, 2005.

I knew August Wilson casually. We met when he became a member of the New Dramatists organization while I was on the admissions committee. Periodically when he was in New York we would meet at a Howard Johnson's restaurant on Broadway to eat ice cream and talk about boxing. I moved to Arizona and hadn't seen him for some time. Then, in 1997, he came to Phoenix for the local premiere of his play *7 Guitars*. There was to be a talkback Q&A with the audience after the show. I was asked to introduce August and host the event. This occasioned a brief reunion. We met for lunch and talked about a variety of things, touching on the speech he

4

gave at Princeton in 1996 entitled, "The Ground on Which I Stand." This monologue is a remembrance of that conversation.

 Just Chattin'

August Wilson, age fifty-two, is sitting at a small table, talking to a friend.

August:

I don't want to talk about the controversy [*his historic and controversial "Ground on Which I Stand" speech given at Princeton University in 1996*] at this thing, because this isn't the time or the place. Everywhere I go, that is what people want to talk about. It usually is stirred up by an article in the local paper written by somebody that doesn't understand the situation and always ends up distorting it in all kinds of ways. Besides that, it occupies center stage, and the real reason I'm visiting the theatre or the organization gets lost or forgotten. So for those and other reasons I'm not gonna talk about it today and maybe you can announce it just at the start.

Pause.

All kinds of people, white and black, ask me why I spoke out at Princeton like I did. They all want to know about that place and that time. It was like they were accusing me of having bad manners. The truth is it had been on my mind for some time. And I had been meaning to talk about it for a while but I kept putting it off and putting it off, telling myself, "This ain't the right time," or "This ain't the right place." . . . Then it came to me one day that no place or time will ever be right, and if it was going to be said I just better go on and say it. So that's what I did. The next time I had a public platform I made my statement.

Pause.

The white press and the theatre establishment tell me I got no cause to complain, because the theatre has treated me well. Better than any black playwright they can think of or remember. And they like to point out that they've given me all kinds of prizes too. So I guess as far as they are concerned I should be grateful and keep my mouth shut. Well, I am grateful. I know how lucky I am. But I also know how hard I worked to earn what it is I am getting. But to tell me that I can't talk about what I see is to limit my freedom of speech. So no matter how you look at it, that can't be right.

Pause.

In a lot of ways I feel like Paul Robeson felt when they told him that same thing all those years ago. Robeson said, "I don't measure success in terms of myself, when all around me I see injustice and mistreatment being done to my race." . . . I see the same thing with our black theatre artists. They're either being ghettoized or homogenized. So on one side our culture is being pushed into the shadows, and the other side is being watered down so much that one day we won't be able to recognize it as our own anymore.

They tell me that I should be happy and thrilled to be produced so often. That I speak for Black America every time my plays are produced. But one person can't speak for a whole race of people. There are other black voices and other black playwrights whose work needs to be seen and voices need to be heard. They never put that stuff on white playwrights. Never said that Eugene O'Neill or Tennessee Williams spoke for the white population of America. But they always put it on us. "One nigger at a time" is what they're saying whether they want to admit it or not.

Well let's forget about that for a day. Let's celebrate the fact that I am here and you are here and that the play's getting done. And that we got some damn fine actors making the whole thing come alive in all kind of ways.

Pause.

I ain't seen you since New York all them years ago. I still go to HoJo's whenever I'm in town. I love that pistachio nut ice cream of theirs.

Problem is I always eat too much, but I don't care. And wherever I go, I always look to see if there's a place where I can find that ice cream. Sometimes I find it, but for some reason it's never as good as the one they have in New York. I don't know why. Maybe it's because I discovered it there.

Pause.

I like to write in cafes. There's this little coffee shop I go to, where I sit at little table all by myself with my pad. The people know me, so they just come over, say hello, and then leave. I sit sometimes for hours listening to the music that's playing and watching the people come in and out. Then I start to write whatever it is that comes into my head. Sometimes it's a poem or story that one guy's telling another. Whatever it is, I let it take me to wherever it's going to go and for however long it wants. That's how it works for me. With everybody it's different, I know that. (*Looking at his watch*) We better go do this thing, it's getting near time.

BASS REEVES
(?–1910)

One of the blind spots in American history has to do with the presence and function of African Americans in the Old West. After the Civil War there were many black cowboys who distinguished themselves in a variety of ways. People like Nat Love (aka Deadwood Dick), Jesse Stahl, Bill Pickett, Isom Dot, and Bass Reeves.

Bass Reeves was considered by many to be possibly the best man-hunter and marshal in the entire West. He started out as a slave who accompanied his owner, Confederate Colonel George Reeves, as a body servant to Arkansas, where it is said he developed and mastered his skill with firearms. After the war he traveled across the border to the Indian Nations and lived among the Creek Indians and learned to speak their language fluently. In time he learned the languages of all the Five Civilized Tribes (Cherokee, Choctaw, Creek, Seminole, and Chickasaw).

The year was 1875. Outlaws were rampant throughout the area, and Hanging Judge Parker was assigned to bring law and order to the large expanse of the territory. One of the many people he hired was Bass Reeves as deputy marshal. He hired him for several good reasons. Reeves was fast and accurate with a gun, knew the territory intimately, spoke all the Native languages, and was known to be fearless in battle.

Reeves served as deputy marshal from 1875–1901 and in that time arrested more than three thousand men and women, among them many of the most feared and dangerous outlaws of the time. He is also said to have killed fourteen men, all in self-defense.

Reeves was a big man (six foot two) with a boisterous outgoing personality. He died in Oklahoma in 1910. He was inducted into the National Cowboy Hall of Fame in 1992.

◙ Knowing the Territory ◙

Bass Reeves is dressed neatly but somewhat colorfully in cowboy garb, including a black hat. He has his pistol slung on his side and is talking to some young deputy recruits. The year is 1894; he is fifty-four.

Bass:

The first thing you got to understand is when you point a pistol as somebody you have to expect that he gon' be pointing one at you. . . . When you fire a bullet at a man, that man gon' be firing one at you sure as heaven is up and hell is down. Outlaws and criminals like their lifes just as much as you. Some of them even more. When you spent time going after them and is successful in catching up to where they is hiding and you got them like rats in the corner, you got to expect that they can do what rats do. They can come after you and come after you wild. And when they do, they only have one thing in mind, to kill you dead, dead, dead. So's you can never come after them again. With these kinda people the only advantage you have most of the time is smarts. 'Cause most people that take up the criminal life usually ain't smart at all. They usually is dumb bastards, which is why they had to take up with crime in the first place. So you being smarter can usually figure ways of tricking them so that you can get the upper hand. But the trick in going after outlaws is not to underestimate anything they'll do and be prepared for it.

Pause.

I been successful at marshalling because before I go after a man I study everything I can find out about his ways as much as I can. Now I never learned to read, but that don't stop me none. I get other people to read the newspaper stories about who it is I is going after. And I also try to talk to people who might have known the outlaw about his outlaw ways. After I find out as much as I can about him, then I plan my approach and who I wants to be when I go into his territory. Sometimes I goes in as a tramp or a farmer. Other times it might be as a preacher or cowpuncher. Sometime I even go in as a gentleman with shiny boots and spurs. I always get the clothes that make me look like the person I am saying I is. After that I choose a name for people to call me and the weapons I is gon' use when I gets the outlaw in my range.

Now you gotta understand that killin' ain't the first thing on my mind. I prefer, if I have the choice, to bring in a man alive. If he can move on his own it's a lot easier than lifting and lugging some dead body all over the place. But you gotta be prepared for anything, because most of these desperados don't give you no selection.

Take for example that time I went after Bad Bob Dozier. Now he was a smart one. A lot smarter than the average criminal. You see, before he turned outlaw he was a successful farmer and business-man. Why he turned to banditry don't nobody know. Maybe the devil just told him to do it and he obeyed. And once he did he was as successful at outlawry as he was at farming.

What made him so successful is that he was unpredictable. He never do the same crime twice. One time he would rob a stage, another hold up a poker game, ambush travelers, rustle cattle, sell stolen horses, or rob banks. You couldn't tell what he was up to or what he was going to do next. And wily man that he was, he cov-ered a lot of ground.

Lot a marshals went after him. None was successful. Some even got theirselves killed. The price on his head was good and I wanted to get him. I wanted to get him bad. So I studied everything I could about the man before setting out. I practiced up on my shooting too. You see, the way I see it, when you go after a man like Dozier you gotta be prepared in every way you can. So although I always been a good shot and quick on the pull, I practiced so I could be even sharper and quicker.

For months and months I went after him and sometimes even got close. But somehow he always managed to slip through my fin-gers. For nearly three years off and on it was like that with him and me. I went after the man but couldn't catch him. It was like the game of cat and mouse. I was the cat he was the mouse, but the mouse was winning all the way. I gotta say that after all my success with other outlaws it was very discouraging that this most-wanted son of a dog was eluding me.

Then one day I got secret word that he was in the territory, mov-ing around from here to there. I decided to go after him again. This time I only took one other person with me, a capable deputy named Holmes. We moved around kinda easy and made some inquiries. Then we moved around some more. Somehow we musta made too many inquiries, because Dozier got wind of us and went on the move. We tracked him to the upper Cherokee Nation and into an area where there was a lot of rocks and trees. Just as we were beginning to get a bead on him, the sky suddenly turned black with a loud roar of thunder and some hard flashes of lighting coming down. Rain just poured over everything. It was coming down so hard we couldn't see nothing and couldn't hear nothing either. Then outta nowhere a bullet come chasing in, putting a hole in the brim of the hat I was wearing. When the lighting flash I thought I seen a man in a tree, but he was gone in an instant. I pointed the tree out to Holmes and he fired off some rounds. But nothing happened. The rain and the storm was too much. We had to take cover in a little cave that was nearby.

Pause.

Hours later the weather stopped and the sun came out again. Quiet like, we wandered out again, stepping in puddles and slipping on rocks. Holmes fell down a slide and I was just about to help him when a bullet from somewhere behind rip the ground close to me. I fell on my back and just lay there with my hand on my pistol. Holmes called to me but I refused to answer. I just lay there as still as I could. I must have been there around a half hour or so when Mr. Dozier, convinced I was dead, come out of his hiding place and walked up to look me over. He has his pistol out, but down at his side. I waited until he was so close that I knew I couldn't miss, then I sat up and said to him, "Drop it!" . . . Don't you know that son-of-a-bastard raised his gun hand and fired at me. He missed and I got him. Got him in the neck. He stood and coughed for a moment, then stumbled a few steps, clutching his neck, and then hit the ground dead. And that was the end of Bad Bob Dozier.

As marshal in this territory there's gonna be a lot of deadly men you'll have to go after. My advice is, be prepared and expect the worst.

They like to say that us colored ain't much good for anything except cooking food and cleaning manure. But I can tell you some things we real good at. One of them is riding and tracking and getting our prey when we sets our minds to it. And if anybody got any doubts about that, tell them to ask the scores of men we already put in jail. Or look at the graves of the men we put in the ground and if any of them can talk, they will tell you that they never want to see a dark man on their trail ever again. Especially if that man happen to be yours truly, Bass Reeves.

BOOKER T. WASHINGTON
(1856–1915)

Booker T. was born to a mulatto slave and an unknown white man. Since he didn't know his father, he had no last name for many years. When he entered school, he took the first name of the man his mother married, a slave named Washington Ferguson, as his last name. Thus Booker Taliaferro became Booker T. Washington.

After working as a coal miner and a houseboy, he enrolled at the Hampton Agricultural Institute, where he was taught and mentored by Samuel Armstrong, a strong opponent of slavery. After graduating from Hampton, Booker T. taught for a while, and then, at the suggestion of Armstrong, became the head of a shabby school called the Tuskegee Negro Normal Institute. Under his leadership the school expanded, and its reputation for excellence became well known. Washington's reputation as a black leader also grew, to the point that he was consulted by businessmen and Presidents in reference to race matters. In 1901, he published his autobiography, *Up from Slavery*. The book is still in print today.

 The Final Key

Booker T. Washington, age thirty-three, is at a podium addressing a group of incoming students. The year is 1889.

Booker T.:

Education is the final key to freedom. Everything else has been gotten, more or less, but this we have to get for ourselves. Ladies and gentlemen if you don't remember anything else I say this morning please remember that. *Education is the final key to freedom.*

Pause.

Education has been for me the cleansing baptismal water, the guiding star that leads to the promised land, and the bright sunshine that shows you the way. Before I discovered education, I was like one lost in a dark wilderness, erratically going in many directions only to find out that I was moving in one big circle, going nowhere. Fortunately I was young enough to discover what was happening to me, and with the help of some very wonderful people I was able to do something about it.

Let us start from the beginning. I was born a slave. I knew who my mother was, but not my father, therefore I had no last name. And I did not acquire one till my mother married a fellow slave, Washington Ferguson. He became my stepfather. When I discovered that I legally needed a last name to function like everyone else, I took his first name. I liked the ring of it—Washington.

My introduction to the world and value of education came while I was working as a houseboy in the home of General Lewis Ruffner. Prior to that I had worked as a salt packer, coal miner, and ditch digger. My education, such as it was, was sporadic. I could read and write my name, but that was about it. I could count a little too. But it was in General Ruffner's house, encouraged by his generous and kindly wife, that I began to fully appreciate what an education could do for me.

At age sixteen, this was in 1872, I walked a great distance to enter the Hampton Agricultural Institute and was lucky enough to be personally tutored by one of the greatest men I have ever encountered: Mr. Samuel Armstrong. This noble gentleman saw something in me worthy of cultivating and supporting and did so to the utmost of his abilities, even going so far as to persuade some very well off men to pay the tuition for my education. But by far the greatest, the very greatest gift that Mr. Armstrong bestowed upon me was to point out the importance of developing a strong moral character and the value of a sensible, practical education.

In this world there is what is called book learning, where one is educated in languages, sciences, and mathematics. Then there is practical learning, where one is instructed in the professions that allow people such as us, the newly freed population of this country, to become self-sufficient, earn a decent living, and acquire our rightful place in society. The emphasis of the Hampton Institute was on the dignity of manual labor. There we learned the practical and technical skills that working with our hands required. And we were taught to be proud of those skills. For people that are starting out with nothing, book learning is a luxury and practical learning is a necessity.

I learned my lesson well from Mr. Armstrong and the Institute, and when my time was over I returned to my home in Malden, Virginia, an educated man. I found work at the local school and remained there for three years, until Mr. Armstrong offered me a job teaching practical learning to the Indians. A few years later, 1880 to be exact, Mr. Armstrong recommended me for a position as the principal teacher of a new school that was being opened, the Tuskegee Negro Normal Institute. It opened on July 4, 1888, and our facilities consisted of one not very strong or reliable building that was owned by a church. Our annual budget was also miniscule. But it was a start. And I knew if we were sensible about it and didn't try to push too hard or too fast, things would get better. So I designed a curriculum, and we began to take in students. We taught some academic subjects but placed our major emphasis on vocational training. Our students leaned masonry, carpentry, leather craft, and cabinet making. They learned to do those jobs well. But most importantly they learned to be proud of themselves and their abilities.

Pause.

In a little over eight years we were able to grow from a shabby makeshift series of shacks with an enrollment of less than thirty to this thriving establishment that sits on five hundred and forty acres of land that we own. And we boast an enrollment of just over four hundred students. But the greatest achievement of all in my mind is the fact that this school was built by the students themselves. It was built out of their talent, labor, tenacity, and pride. It wasn't easy. Nothing worth having is ever gotten easily. Everyone worked long hours, starting from eight in the morning and usually finishing at nine-thirty or ten at night. There were complaints, there were reversals, there were times we all doubted it would ever be done. But we persevered, and when it was finished, when we opened the doors and took our first step into the new building, some of us wept. We wept because we knew that it was the beginning of a new era for the education of us Negroes in this country. We also wept because we knew that this building, this institution, symbolizes and stands as a monument to what downtrodden people can do if they are sensible, practical, committed, determined, and proud. It is said that "faith can move mountains," but it can also be said that pride, the right kind of pride, can build institutions that last. Institutions that define the strength and moral character of our people.

And what is the foundation of all this? Education. Education that tells us that we don't have to loaf around on the streets or in gambling houses and bars. That we don't have to stand in charity lines fighting for pittances or chase after political messiahs who make promises they never deliver. Education, practical education, makes us independent, self-reliant, and strong.

Pause.

In 1872 in order for me to get to the Hampton Agricultural Institute, because I had no others means of transportation, I was forced to walk nearly five hundred miles. But I remember all during that long journey telling myself that it was worth it. Because I had the feeling that to get into that school and be allowed to study would be about the same as getting into paradise. I wasn't wrong. It was a paradise of the mind, a paradise of the spirit. You are all here to be educated. Value it. Why? Because as I said in the beginning, *education is the final key to freedom.*

CHARLES "BUDDY" BOLDEN
(1877–1931)

Bolden is a figure shrouded in fact and legend. Considered to be the First Man of Jazz, or more accurately, the first musician to give jazz (or *jass* as they called it in those days) widespread popularity, Buddy Bolden's story is curious. For a man who is credited as the father of an important musical movement and as a person who was extremely popular (for a short time—1900–1905), virtually nothing was written about him. All that is known is that he was born in New Orleans in 1877, played the cornet, was the first popular jazz musician anyone could remember, was diagnosed as insane in 1907, and spent the last twenty-four years of his life institutionalized. He died in 1931, at age fifty-four, unaware that the "jassy" music he'd just about invented had flourished and developed into America's most indigenous art form.

Because so little is written about Bolden and how his music evolved, I wanted to tell more. I also wanted to have someone other than Buddy do it, hence the sort of mythical character I created for "Witness to the Starting."

 My Own Private Blues

Buddy Bolden, age twenty-six, is sitting on a chair, a bottle on the floor and his cornet next to it. He's been indoors for three days and looks somewhat disheveled.

Buddy:

People is starting to copy the way I play. All over town you hear them talking 'bout Buddy Bolden kinda music. King Bolden music. And every damn musician that hear us steal something. That's all they come by now to do. Steal. This is turning out to be a city full of thieves, and all you can tell me is to pay them no mind? They taking the food from my table and the music from my horn, and I don't know what to do about it. I could bust somebody's face and kick somebody's butt, and that's what I'm going to do if it don't stop. Yeah, that's what I'm going to do.

He takes a long drink from the bottle, sits and thinks for a little. Then he begins singing softly.

Thought I heard Buddy Bolden say
We need a new kind of music.
Take the old stuff away
Rag it up, jass it up
Take it away
Yeah—that's what Mr. Bolden say.

Hattie had the baby. Refused to let me see it, can you believe that? I can't see my own baby. Say I'm a no-account, no-character lowlife who don't deserve to have no child. Say she don't want the boy growing up like me. I tried to see him over and over again but every time I get close to the house something stop me, and I can't get any closer. I try and this thing push me back. I mean hard. It push me back hard.

I know you don't believe me. Or maybe you think it's the liquor talking. But it's true. I swear to God, it's true. What you don't know, you see. . . . What you don't know is that Hattie got powers. Voodoo powers she bring from up the river. Powers she get from her grandmother. She told me so. Said she was going to put a spell on the house and a spell on me, too. Other people tell me she been working on it every time she get a chance. When we was together she was always doing stuff on other people. I used to pay it no mind, but now she turning it on me. . . . That's why everybody stealing my music. That's why I'm having trouble playing it, too. You didn't know that. I didn't tell you.

I went in the other day to practice with the boys. Nothing big, just wanted to try a couple new tunes. It was like I never played before. Every note come out wild and wrong. The harder I tried the worst it got. After a while Lou said it was no use, we better call it a day. I told him it was Hattie, she is the one putting a spell on me. He wouldn't believe it. Lou never want to believe anything he can't touch or see. Said I was tired because I was up and drinking all night. I been up and drinking for three days and three nights, he didn't know that. But it don't affect me that way. I could always play the horn. I can always make the music happen. That's why they call me King Bolden. . . . No, no. This was the first time and I know it got something to do with Hattie. I don't care what nobody say, I know that for a fact.

Takes another drink.

I'm starting to get the headaches again, and all that stuff the doctor give me ain't helping. Only thing that helps is taking a lot of this stuff and going to sleep. And staying asleep until the devil stop stomping around in my head. I tell that to the boys but they don't understand. They think I'm jiving. Think I'm using it as an excuse not to show up. Lou say Sam is upset and talking about not wanting to give me my share. But I am the band. The band is me. Even when I ain't there I's the one the people come to see. I's the reason the band even got any booking. They just jealous that's all. Jealous because I'm the one everybody come to hear. Not Jimmy, not Willie, not Jeff or Lou—me, King Bolden—me.

I ain't been outta this room for three days, you know why? Mama say there's a man with a gun looking for me. Man say I do it with his wife and give her the disease, she do it with him, now he got the disease. So he blame me. Only one thing wrong. I don't know the man or his wife. So that man blaming me for something I ain't done. Got enough trouble with the women around me, don't need to go after no stranger. Especially no married stranger. But that man don't want to hear. Mama tried to talk to him, but he wasn't listening. Got only one thing in mind. Want to put a bullet in the heart of the man he think ruined his wife.

I ain't going out. If it take forever, I ain't going out. Let him kill another Buddy Bolden. Got a whole lot of other Charles Boldens in New Orleans. Let him kill one a them and let me be.

You the only one I can talk to. The only one I can trust. You think I'm wrong wanting to see my son? Everybody get to pick their boy up, hold him in their arms, and look at the smile on his face. Why can't I be the same? Why do I have to have a woman who hate me putting spells everyplace I go?

The music I play, they call it ratty music, darkie music, low-down music, noisy music, no music. Now everybody want to take it and claim it for their own.

He takes another drink and begins to sing again.

I thought I heard Buddy Bolden say
da, da, da, da, da, da, da . . . (*stops*)

You think this is the end of me, don't you? Think you seeing the finish of Buddy Bolden, the king. You wrong, pal. You wronger than wrong. This is just the beginning of a new season and a new day. The music gon' flow, the sun gon' be shining, and all the people gon' be out laughing and eating and listening to all that music. And I'm going to be there, playing up a storm. Oh yeah, I'm going to be blowing like I never blowed before. And you know what the people gon' say? "Oh, that's just Buddy calling his children home. Buddy the king, blowing his self out through that horn."

Yeah, that's what they're going to say when they hear me play again. . . . Yeah, that's exactly what they're going to say.

He goes back to the bottle, takes a long sip as the lights fade.

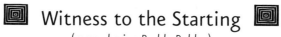 Witness to the Starting

(remembering Buddy Bolden)

A black man, over forty but seeming ageless, dressed in rags, stands on an empty stage.

Man:

Yeah, yeah—so it went something like this.

True story. No lie. This is a true story.

The boy's mother's name was Alice. Little skinny bit of a thing. Worked down the way as a maid for some white folks. Don't remember their name anymore. Had a nice-size house down on Washington. But that don't matter. Her name was Alice and she was twenty-two.

His old man's name was Westmore. Westy we used to call him. Westy Bolden, a drayman with a cart. Used to carry stuff all over town if you pay him. Damn cart and the horse that used to drag it always look like it was about to fall apart. Bolden didn't look all that much better, but they would always manage to make it somehow. Him and that horse and that cart. But that was his old man. Westy Bolden, twenty-six years old.

The year was 1877. And the place was New Orleans, Louisiana. They writing all them books now and they getting the whole thing all wrong. Especially the dates. Charles "Buddy" Bolden—the man they now calling the father of jazz—was born on September 6, 1877. And I should know. I witnessed the whole thing.

Who am I? Well that ain't none of your business. Just go on sipping your drinks and looking at the paintings and tell yourself that I am one crazy colored man who just wandered in off the street who don't know what he's talking about.

That I am just some kind of derelict walking the streets babbling about all kinds a stuff. Because the truth, the truth is hard to believe. But I'll tell it to you once. Just once, then you can go back to being ignorant if you like.

Who am I? I am a time traveler. I travel through decades and sometimes through centuries. I witness things and come back or go forward to talk about it. Why? Because I like to, that's all. A man's got to talk to somebody sometime. Can't keep everything in his head. Make you crazy after a while. So, I visit folks, tell them things, and then I move on. Don't come back twice or three times. Just once. And that's it. I'm gone.

Anyway, we were talking about Buddy Bolden. Inventor of jazz. Father of jazz. King of jazz. Or whatever it is they now calling him. And I'm here to tell you they got it all wrong. Most of them.

See, when a person becomes famous, then everybody and his uncle want to claim that they used to know him when. And what they do is make up a lot of lies just to prove that all of it is so. And them investigators from the Library of Congress and everyplace else listen to those lies and put them in their books. And that's how the whole thing about jazz got confused.

First of all in them days they didn't call it jazz. They called it jass. J-A-S-S. Jassy music colored folks in a certain part a New Orleans used to play and listen to—dance to sometimes— coming outta the roots of ragtime, but with its own kind a raggy beat. We used to call it jassing the music. You know, making up your own stuff 'cause you know people done already know the tune. So you jabba and jive and mess around. You jass up the music. You follow what I's saying?

Show them a little something for me, fellows please.

A group in the wings does some jazz improv.

That's what I'm talking about. Everybody at the time was doing it. Every good band, that is. But Buddy is the one who get credit for it. And maybe that's how it should be. He is the one who pulled it all together and made it popular. And because a that whenever people talk about the beginning of jazz—they talk about Buddy Bolden. But like I told you, other people was doing it. Other people was jassing around. You could hear it on Gallatin Street, Calliope, and even on Howard Street, which is where Buddy was born. People was playing it and folks used to move to it. Oh yes, move all night sometimes.

But we got to give some credit to Buddy. He come outta nowhere. Son of a maid and a garbage mover. Father died when the boy was six. Died of pneumonia. Lots of people died from it that year. Westy Bolden was one of them. So the boy grew up with his mother and younger sister, Cora. Alice tried her best, but the boy grew up wild anyway. Always running with bad company. Always peering through windows and seeing things he shoudnt'a been seeing. You know what I mean. Things having to do with womens and mens when they got no clothes on. New Orleans was a rough place in those days. Especially the colored section.

Lord, I could tell you stories about things I done and seen. Stories that would make—but let's forget about that. Let's stick to the subject. The subject is Buddy Bolden. But before we go on, will somebody bring me a glass of water? My throat is dry from talking so much. (*Somebody does*) Thank you. (*He drinks*) Now, like I was saying. The boy growed up wild. Seeing wild things, doing wild things, and listening to wild music. He would hear it on the street, hear it in church, hear it at parades and from marching bands at funerals. Music was everywhere he could turn. And the boy was liking what he was hearing.

Other folks was working and going to church. Buddy was breaking into places and stealing stuff. But he was listening to music and learning how to play. He got his first lesson from Manny Hall, a cook who was seeing his mama. Manny took an interest in the boy and taught him how to play the horn.

See, Manny used to be a musician once upon a time. He used to play the cornet. And although he wasn't playing anymore, he kept his horn, and that's what he used to teach the boy. Buddy was a quick study. Or maybe he had a natural aptitude, I don't know. But soon he was playing better than Manny and was even doing a little reading of sheet music too. All this was around 1890 to 1894. Buddy was playing when he had time, stealing whenever he got the chance, and messing with girls and older women too in intimate ways.

The boy was growing up fast and there wasn't nothing that Alice could do about it. Barbershops were the place where wild boys hung out so's they could talk to gamblers, highlife boys, cut pockets, whore runners, musicians, and pimps. In fact, barbershops was the place where musicians used to get their jobs out of. Anybody looking to hire a band was to go to the barbershops and the barber would get them one.

Number one place in the area, for colored folks, was Louis Jones Barbershop. That's where Buddy used to hang out. Some books say he used to cut hair too. But that wasn't so. Buddy Bolden wasn't never a barber. All he did was hang out in the place. And that's how he got his first musical job. Through hanging out.

He couldn'ta been more'n fifteen or sixteen, but he was out there playing and playing hard.

A brief musical interlude.

After the sessions everybody would go out and drink. Get their heads bad. And after that—well you got your imaginations, you know what folks do when the liquor gets good and the hour gets late. And Buddy wasn't any different. Buddy did his share. Even more than his share.

At sixteen he was living with a woman. At nineteen he was living with two. At twenty, a woman name Hattie had a child for Buddy. A boy. They called him Buddy Junior. Buddy's mama, Alice, didn't like Hattie. Said she was a lowlife and a whore. But Hattie said she was reformed. The only person she slept with now was Buddy and that wasn't for money, but love.

He pauses to smile and consider the significance or irony of that remark; maybe a brief snatch of music is heard.

Buddy was the father of a child now. But he was becoming the father of something else that he didn't even know about. And that something was jazz. It didn't have a name, or even a form. But it was music. Something new folks hadn't heard before. And Buddy was the one playing and experimenting with it.

You see, by this time Buddy had his own band and they was playing a bunch a places. The Old Mission Hall, the Big Twenty-Five Bar, Casey's Rhythm Room, Jack's Korner, and the Cut Bell Lounge. Most of them were ratholes, but that didn't matter. Women were there and the places was paying money, so Buddy played them. Plus Johnny Robichaux's band was the one playing all the nicer places like the Globe Hall and the Odd Fellow Ballroom. His music was refined and civilized. Not ragged up and jassy like Buddy's.

Still the word was getting out 'bout the big noise coming outta those ratholes. And that big noise was Buddy. Buddy, who folks was already starting to call the king on account a the way he drink and carry himself. But mostly on account a the way he play.

Every Sunday when the weather was warm you could find him up in Lincoln Park playing in a cutting contest. Cutting contests were a kind of a game musicians liked to play where they would get up on a stand and try to outplay each other. Since most of them was horn players, it was really a blowing contest. Those fools would get up on that stand one by one and blow till their hearts and breaths give out and the notes turned sour. It was an Olympic contest for musicians, and the folks used to love it.

At first Buddy joined in just for fun. But as time went by you could tell he was serious. That boy blew and blew and then continued blowing. Next thing you know he wasn't stopping to take too much breath. He just kept on blowing. Folks from all over the park stop to see what was going on.

I ain't talking about twenty or thirty. I'm talking about two maybe three hundred people, could' a been even four hundred, far as I know. They all gather 'round. It was something to see. All these black faces gathered 'round and shouting, "Blow, Buddy, blow!" And as loud as they would shout it, he would play that horn even louder. And I ain't talking notes, I'm talking sweet music. Music that was like liquid fire and alcohol moving through your veins.

And that boy was sweating, but it was like the devil was in his soul. He just couldn't stop. And the folks wouldn't let him. The music rushed out and we all sucked it in. It was like electricity was all around. Women was rubbing sexy parts of their bodies and breathing hard. And the men, most of the ones I notice, including myself, was in a daze. We didn't know what the hell was going on, but we knowed it was something special. Something unique that we would be telling our grandchildren about in years to come. Don't ask me how long it went. Some book say three hours, others say four. All I know is that it seemed like forever, but it also seemed like one minute too.

Then when it was over, everything just stopped. Buddy, with that horn, who seemed to grow so tall that he was blocking out the sun, suddenly was this shriveled-up boy, covered from head to toe in sweat, looking like he had been in a fight and somebody had given him a terrible beating.

I don't remember anybody talking much. We were all in too much of a daze. But after that there was no question as to who the king a New Orleans music was. Women started to ask if they could carry his horn. And kids would take his coat and follow him around the neighborhood like he was Moses leading them to the promised land.

Play some music fellows, let me catch my breath. The excitement of that remembrance has left me a little short of breath.

The musicians play.

Now, it's a funny thing about being at the beginning or the start of anything. Being the father of a movement, if you want to call it that. Buddy didn't have an inkling. Not a notion or anything like that. All that boy know is that him and his band was playing music that people like to hear. And that was that. He was blowing up a storm and the folks would come. From all over the place they would come to crowd the halls and hear Buddy play.

He would say, "I know my peoples is here, 'cause I can smell 'em." And he wrote a little song called "The Funky Butt Blues," later called "Buddy Bolden's Blues." And it goes like this:

> I thought I heard Buddy Bolden say
> Your dirty, nasty, stinking butt
> Take it away
> Funky butt, stinky butt
> Take it away
> And let Mr. Bolden play.
> Thought I heard Mr. Lincoln shout
> Close up them plantations
> Let the black folks out
> Close 'em up, shut 'em down
> That's what he shout
> And—let them black folks out.

It was kind of a calling card song and everybody knowed it. Used to sing along when Buddy played it. Years later somebody cleaned it up and called it "The St. Louis Tickle." But everybody knowed it by its real name: "The Funky Butt Blues." Used to have other songs too. Most a them rough and dirty. But "Funky Butt Blues" was the calling card.

Now Buddy had another way he used to call the folks out. Say he was playing some place, and there wasn't too much of a crowd on account that it wasn't advertised too good. All Buddy would do is point his horn out the window and blow his notes out in the quiet Louisiana air. He would blow them so sweet and so loud that all the folks would hear and come to fill up the place.

Jelly Roll Morton, who lied about so many people and so many things, wasn't lying when he called Buddy "the blowinist man since the angel Gabriel." The cornet is a tough instrument to play, but Buddy blow it so loud that folks would say they could hear him forty miles away. A lot of that is legend. But most of it is fact. Cold, hard fact.

The band was popular, Buddy was the king, and the money was rolling in. But Buddy's private life was falling apart. Hattie, the woman he was living with, who was the mother of his son, didn't hardly ever see him. Buddy would stay out for days shacked up and drunk. And when he did come home he would just sleep all day then go out at night to play and mess around. Hattie, who had become saved, talked to him about it. But Buddy would curse her and tell her to leave him alone. When she couldn't take it any longer she upped and left, taking their son with her. This was a blow to Buddy, because he loved that boy. But Hattie wouldn't let him visit or go anywhere near the boy.

It was around this same time that Buddy started getting his headaches. Today we call them migraines, but in them days folks used to call it the thumping thunders. And Buddy would get them thunders real bad. They would last all day and was like to split his head open. Wasn't no medicine that could do any good, so Buddy used to drink everything he could get his hands on to chase away the pain. So he was a man in two kinds of agony. Pain pounding inside his head. And liquor burning right through his body all the way to his soul.

This condition would go on for days, sometimes even a week. And when he was like that, Buddy couldn't play anything. The band would have to go out on their own. But the bad thing was, half the time they didn't know where they was scheduled to play or what gigs they had. Buddy kept all that in his head and would forget to tell it to the band. Louis Jones, at the barber shop, became the man who would keep tabs on where the band was to play because Buddy just couldn't be trusted. When the man was well, everything was fine. But them headaches come, he wasn't any good to anybody, least of all himself.

I'm dry again. I should have something strong, but I'll save that for later.

He drinks water. Perhaps a brief snatch of music.

After the first wave of these headache attacks Buddy slowed down. He had to. His mother and sister came over to nurse him. They even got him to going back to church for a while. He would play at night and seek the Lord in the morning. Maybe through quietness and prayer, he would find a way out of the thumping thunders.

This is where he met Nora, a quiet church woman. And pretty as the sun is bright. Everybody warned her about Buddy. Told her he was a whoremaster and a drunk. That he was no good. And that he would treat her bad. But Nora didn't hear any of it. What she saw was a man she was in love with and that was that.

They got married on a Sunday and for a while Buddy did try to settle down. He tried real hard, but it wasn't to be. Buddy wasn't cut out to be a husband. He was a wild man and a musician. That's how God made him, and that's how he had to be.

The red-light district in New Orleans was a rough place. On weekend nights there was killings on top of killings. And then there was the cathouses where everything God frowns on went on for twenty-four hours a day in all kinds a places from the bedrooms to the stairwells and the hallways and the kitchens. And even in the parlors.

The women had tricks and the men would pay with every dime they had. Gambling and doping was big in them places too. Everything was so wide open that later on when Alderman Sidney Story, who hated jazz, tried to reform things, the place come to be known as Storyville. But that was a few years later. Now it was just wide open and Buddy was in the middle, taking it all in.

In the year 1900, the turn of the century, the Buddy Bolden

Band was the most popular in the area. The only one that was even close was the John Robichaux Band. They was considered more refined. But the rough people loved Buddy's noise. Loved it so much that other people started to copy what he was doing. Not only copied it, but improved on it too.

This made Buddy crazy. Just to keep ahead he was blowing louder and harder. Something inside told him he had broken new ground. Marked some musical real estate as his own. But now he was having trouble holding on to it. And if he didn't, just as quickly as it came, it would go away.

The other fellows in the band told him not to sweat it so much. There was room enough for everybody. But Buddy didn't want to hear that. He was the king and he wanted to be king forever.

Ironically the harder he tried, the worse he played. Sometimes the other guys in the band would have to stop and ask him what the hell he was doing. "You're turning us into noise makers instead of a band." But Buddy didn't care. He just kept on pushing and pushing. And if anybody gave him an argument he would turn violent.

It got so bad that one day the rest of the band told him to go home. They didn't need him anymore. Buddy tried to argue and fight, but the boys had made their minds up. He wasn't helping the band. He was hurting it.

For awhile Buddy tried to start another band, but nobody would play with him.

On Labor Day in 1906 Buddy tried to play in a marching band and was playing so bad that they had to push him out of the parade.

His headaches were bad, but his drinking was even worse. Nora couldn't put up with it anymore, so she, with Buddy's second child, a girl named Bernadine, moved in with her mother. Only his own mother, Alice, would try to deal with him. But he would go crazy and attack her, so she would have to leave too. But she always came back. Until the day of March 13, 1907, when he broke a water pitcher over her head. After doing that he attacked his horn and was locked up in the police station as drunk and crazy. On June fifth of that same year he was moved to the State Insane Asylum in Jackson, Louisiana. Charles "Buddy" Bolden lived in that state asylum from 1907 to 1931.

On November fourth of 1931, at the age of fifty-four, Buddy Bolden died of cerebral arterial sclerosis. People at his small funeral were Cora, his sister; Louis Jones, the barber; Nora, his wife; and Bernadine, his beautiful twenty-year-old daughter. He was buried next to his mother, Alice, who had died just a few months earlier. She had never given up on her son. And had been his most frequent visitor in all the years he was locked up. "He blew his mind out through his horn," folks liked to say. But what happened to Buddy no one can say for sure.

But in 1938, seven years after his death, the music called jazz that Buddy pioneered and popularized became recognized as a distinctive musical form. It grew up while he was institutionalized. And people like Louis Armstrong, Sidney Bechet, and yes, Ferdinand "Jelly Roll" Morton, along with many others, had turned that jassy rag stuff into an indigenous American art.

In 1942, eleven years after his passing, through the memories and writings of people who was there, Charles "Buddy" Bolden— that wild man with the horn—was acknowledged to be the founding father of jazz.

One quick story and then I'll take my leave.

I told you I was witness to all of this and that was true. One day, one Sunday afternoon in May of 1898, a bunch of colored soldiers was getting ready to ship out to Cuba because of the coming war with Spain. A whole bunch a people came out to see the boys off, including Buddy and the band. We was all gathered on the banks of the Mississippi to wave the boys goodbye. Buddy and the band was playing as the boat sailed away. Just as the boat reached the middle of the river, those young soldiers started to dive off and swim back.

When they was asked why, they said Buddy's music was too sweet. They just couldn't go away from it. After that, Buddy was asked by the authorities not to see the boys off anymore.

That's the Buddy I remember. Sweet, hot, and exciting.

Good night to you all.

CORETTA SCOTT KING
(1927–2006)

Mrs. Martin Luther King was born in Marion, Alabama. In 1951, she received a bachelor of arts degree in music and education from Antioch College, in Yellow Springs, Ohio, and went on to earn a bachelor of arts degree in music from the New England Conservatory of Music, in Boston, Massachusetts.

Coretta Scott made her concert debut as a singer in Springfield, Ohio, in 1948. She then gave numerous performances in the United States as well as in India. She was married to the civil rights leader in 1953.

During her married years with MLK she maintained the stability of their family life and actively supported his civil rights initiatives. After his death, she remained vigorously active in the civil rights movement, becoming the president of the Martin Luther King Memorial Center and joining the board of directors of the Southern Christian Leadership Conference. She wrote an autobiography in 1969, *My Life with Martin Luther King*.

 I Remember

Coretta:

The memory is an impolite intruder who hides in the attic of your mind and chooses to come out only at the most inconvenient moments. When you're standing on the street waiting for a bus to come. Or when you're listening to someone and a word they say or phrase they use reminds you of someone or a time long ago. Sometimes it gets triggered by the words of a song or the sound of a special voice.

Time sometimes heals wounds, but it can never replace the loved ones that we've lost. So we're left with memories of the time we spent together. The good and the bad. And those rare quiet moments in between.

Pause.

With the passage of time, Martin has become as controversial in death as he was in life. There are many who will question, distort, exploit, and impugn what he stood for and what he accomplished. We who were close to him know the man he was and we hold his memory dear.

Perhaps for me the happiest memory I have of Martin is in 1964, when we went to Oslo, Sweden, for him to accept his Nobel Prize. Although we knew he had been nominated, his getting it came as a complete surprise.

"This year the prize is worth fifty-four thousand dollars," the reporter said to him. "What do you intend to do with the money, Mr. King?"

"Divide it among the Southern Christian Leadership Conference, the Congress of Racial Equity, the Student Nonviolent Coordinating Committee, the NAACP, the National Council of Negro Women, and the American Foundation on Nonviolence," he answered.

Pause.

The prize was important for it said that Martin's activities were recognized as worthwhile not just here in America, and not just among African American peoples, but by everyone, the world over.

Privately, I was pleased because it told our four children better than I could ever imagine that their father, who had been jailed so many times and had been called a liar, a communist, an Uncle Tom, a criminal, and every other unpleasant name one could think of, had been right after all. And the rightness of his stand had now been universally recognized.

There were so many events and ceremonies to attend. All required formal wear, and Martin, who had been such a dandy when I first met him, found it annoying having to wear a bow tie. The problem was, he didn't know how to tie it.

"Why do I have to wear one of these? Why can't I wear the clip-on kind?" he asked. I explained, in formal wear this was the only kind that was acceptable. "This thing is a pain. It always comes out looking lopsided. The clip-on kind is neat and it's no bother to wear." Finally, I said, "Let me." And I tied it for him. Then he wanted to know: "How'd you learn to tie these things? Have you been sneaking off behind my back taking lessons?" And we laughed. Then he said, "Let's take a quiet moment to reflect how long and how difficult it's been for us to get to this place." We hugged and then we cried a little, because I guess somewhere inside we knew we'd never have a moment like that again.

Then, with his tie straight and a special flower given to him by the children, he went to accept that great honor. He accepted the prize on behalf of the twenty-two million black people in America who were engaged in a mighty battle to end the long night of racial injustice. "I accept this award," he said, "with an abiding faith in America and an audacious faith in the future of mankind."

Martin is gone but the faith he inspired endures. And so do we. Thank you for coming here tonight. And God bless you all.

She exits.

ELIZABETH HUDSON SMITH
(1869–1935)

Elizabeth was called the "Hostess of the West" because she was a renowned cook in the area and built a hotel that has been designated a national landmark. She was born in Alabama and went to college in Chicago, where she became fluent in French and was already establishing a reputation as a very good cook. At twenty-seven, she married William Smith, who worked as a valet for the railroad magnate George Pullman. They moved to Wickenburg, Arizona, in 1897, where she worked as a cook and hostess at the Baxter Hotel. Her reputation became so renowned that the railroad gave her the opportunity to create a hotel as a stop-off point for train passengers headed to California, which she did with the financial support of her mother-in-law. The hotel was called Vernetta.

She also became an integral part of the Wickenburg community, where she founded the first Presbyterian Church, a local community theatre, and championed for Arizona statehood. She also introduced motion pictures to the area by showing them in the backyard of her hotel. Still, her greatest achievement was building and successfully running the Vernetta Hotel, making it the center of the social life in the area.

She divorced her husband in 1912, which is the same year Arizona became a state. Then things began to change. The multiracial community of Wickenburg had become overrun mostly with white Southerners, and ultimately, because of her color, she was ousted from the church she helped to found and ostracized. Although financially well off, she became a recluse in her final years.

Today the Vernetta Hotel is listed on the National Register of Historical Sites and the story of her life is being told in biographies, plays, and video dramatizations.

◼ 🔳 A Monument to Me 🔳 ◼

A bare stage with one antique chair. Elizabeth Hudson Smith, an African American in her early forties, is dressed in period costume.

Elizabeth:

I had never been out West and it was never in my plans. I was born in Alabama, educated at Northwestern in Illinois, and lived in the windy city of Chicago.

My father was an ex-slave named Sales Hudson that Mr. Lincoln and the Civil War freed. And when he heard that great Negro orator Frederick Douglass say, "Education: education, my friends, is the final key to freedom," he took it to heart and insisted that I be college educated. In those days very few people were college educated. And certainly no black woman. But I was. And it has certainly stood me well and made me freer than I ever would have been without it.

While living in Chicago I worked as a teacher, giving lessons in history, English, and French because I had always been good at languages. I don't know why. It was just a gift I was born with.

Then, in 1896, at age twenty-seven, I got married to William Halltree Smith, a good-looking black man who worked off and on as a Pullman porter. And sometimes even as a valet for Mr. Pullman himself.

The plan was for us to settle in Chicago where we had family and friends and start ourselves a family of our own. I was a woman interested in children and teaching them everything I had come to learn through books and study and just being in the world. Then William came home to me one night and said, "Lizzie, we going out West." Now I never liked anybody calling me Lizzie. No, I never liked it at all. But William was my husband, so he was allowed.

"What you mean we going out West?" I asked him. "You mean you're going out, on the train."

"No," he corrected me, "We. I'm going to be the personal valet to Mr. Pullman on this trip. When I told him I had just got married and didn't want to leave my wife so soon, he said: 'Bring her along.'"

Pause.

And that's how it happened that I came out West. Southwest, really. To the land they was calling the Arizona Territory. A wilderness desert full of jackrabbits, rattlesnakes, cactus, mountain ranges, and Indians, Indians, Indians. Also a lot of Chinese people working on the building of railroad tracks. And a lot of white prospectors from all over digging mines looking for copper, silver, and gold.

But I think I need first to talk about Mr. Pullman. He's the one everybody associates with my name. Mr. George Mortimer Pullman. White, rich, and powerful. He was an industrialist, designer of the Pullman Car, and a union breaker. Many people called him an all-round SOB as well. He created the Pullman porters. That gave a lot of colored men work. But most said he was a hard man to work for and almost impossible to like. William, my husband, didn't feel that way at all. "Mr. Pullman ain't worse than any other white man I know. He just got more money. You do your job right, he'll leave you alone. Do it wrong and he'll be all over you all the time."

Well, I guess I must've been doing something right on that long train ride we shared to Arizona, because every night he would stay up and talk to me like I was a student in a class he was teaching. The truth is, he suffered from insomnia and liked to stay up all night drinking brandy and talking. And since I was the only one not working for him on the train, my hours were flexible. So William said that I should sleep daytimes and stay up late to talk to Mr. Pullman and get him anything he needed. That would give William several hours at night to sleep.

Pause.

Pullman hardly asked me for anything except to listen while he went on for hours and hours saying that the only ticket to freedom for Negroes was finances. "They got to get into business and become self-supporting. Stop being dependent on the white man to carry and support you. Stand on your own two feet. And business finances is the only way to achieve that." He said that to me I can't tell you how many times. To the point where I would sometimes fall asleep listening to him talk.

When we got to Arizona, he told me it was "the landscape of opportunity" because it was so "wide open and underdeveloped."

Pause.

We got off at a place called Wickenburg, William and me. Mr. Pullman went on without us because his regular valet was better now. In Wickenburg we planned to stay only a few months and then go back to Chicago. We got a job at a run-down hotel called the Baxter. I did the cooking, and William greeted the customers and served them. In a little over a year we was running the place and keeping it filled with satisfied customers. We didn't own the business but we sure were keeping it going.

Years passed and we forgot all about going back to Chicago. This was our home now. Wickenburg, part of the Arizona Territory that everybody said would soon become a state in the Union.

Eight years passed and we were still going strong at the Baxter. Plus, I had gotten involved in a lot of community work, like helping to build the First Presbyterian Church, forming a local community theatre group, giving cooking lessons, and teaching French like I did in Chicago.

William didn't get into much of that. He liked to drink and gamble a little bit. And he liked to speculate in business. So we didn't have any problems. He was going his way and I was going mine.

Then, in 1905, January it was, two railroad men came to talk to me about building a hotel with a restaurant in it where their passengers could have a nice place to wash up and eat while the train took on water and coal. They didn't want to talk to William. They wanted to talk to me. When I asked them why, they said Mr. Pullman had recommended me. But Mr. Pullman had been dead for eight years already. He died the very year we came out to Wickenburg. They said before he died he told them I was the one they should talk to. "So as you see," they said, "we have been thinking about this for quite some time."

Pause.

The proposition was simple. I would build the hotel, they would provide the customers. The railroad gave me a thousand dollars, and the rest of the money I had to raise.

But before anything was settled, I told them William was my husband and partner. Anything I was involved with, he has to be a part of too. They said fine. And when I told William about it he said, "Lizzie, this is what we've been waiting for. This is a godsend."

For the hotel I wanted only the best. I wanted it to be made of bricks. I wanted it to have two stories with lots of windows for sunlight. And I wanted the restaurant to serve the best food anybody ever tasted. But I needed a plan. But more than that I needed money, money, money.

For a plan I wrote to James Cheighton, an architect in Phoenix. The best money could buy, they said. Then I wrote to Vernetta Smith, William's mother (my mother-in-law) and told her of our plans. She quickly wrote back and said she would mortgage her house to get us the money we needed. When Mr. Cheighton came back with his drawings, I knew we were in business.

The finished hotel, for me, was like a dream come true. Everybody said it was the finest building in Wickenburg. And the railroad men said that the whole thing had surpassed their expectations. They even went so far as to build a boardwalk from the train station right to the front door of the hotel.

Everything was going so well, and I was so busy running the place and working in the community, that I hadn't noticed how me and William were drifting apart. He was working in the hotel but he didn't feel a part of it. Then one day he said he wanted to open a saloon in the back. I didn't think it was a good idea but he insisted. A year later when it failed and I had to close it, he told me he wanted a divorce. We had been married fifteen years and all of a sudden it was over. I still loved William but he was determined to leave. So I bought out his share of the hotel and watched him walk away.

I was so lonely and lost, there was nothing to do but bury myself in work. The case of statehood was being talked about all over. I jumped on the bandwagon. Statehood would mean more people, more commerce, and a more civilized way of living. I was for all that. I joined several women's groups. And there was even a little bit of talk that after statehood was achieved, I might be put up as a candidate for an elected office.

Arizona became the forty-eighth state on February 14, 1912, when President William Taft signed the proclamation. February fourteenth, Valentine's Day. Ironically, it was the same day that I received the final decree of my divorce from William. There was gunfire, fireworks, and all kinds of other events celebrating statehood. And I was right in the middle of it all, celebrating with everybody else.

What I didn't realize at the time was that would be the turning point in my life. It's a bitter thing to look back and see that you miscalculated and misjudged. That you were too busy being smart to realize that you were really being a fool.

It began with the new people moving into town. Southerners mostly. They started building other businesses and getting involved in community affairs. I was a single woman and I was seeing a man. His name was Bill, too. He was colored and I had hired him to play the piano and sing at the hotel. Next thing I knew there were rumors that him and I were running a house of ill repute, with prostitutes at the hotel. When Bill couldn't take it any longer, he decided to leave and advised me to do the same. I refused, reasoning this was just a phase people were going through. After all these people were my friends. They had known me now for nearly twenty years, and knew the kind of person I was.

But things got worse; behind my back I was being called Dusky Belfy and Nigger Lizzie. To my face, people who used to speak warmly to me openly snubbed me. When I realized that there would be no turning back in their attitudes was when I received a note telling me that I was no longer a member of the Presbyterian Church I helped to found.

I still had the Vernetta Hotel and was still running it at a profit. I also had financial interests in a few other business ventures around. Mr. Pullman was right. Money had made me free, free to move away from the slander, calumny, and bigotry of the people I had given so much of myself to. So I bought a farm at the outskirts of town where I could keep an eye on my various investments but I didn't have to deal with the small, narrow people who had turned so abruptly against me.

Today, I have my Bible and my memories. And the faces of those who took the ride with me. Vernetta and Pullman. And especially William, whose love I sacrificed in trying to build a dream out of a wilderness.

But one thing still stands. And it's going to stand for a long, long time. And that is the Vernetta . . . it says, "Elizabeth Hudson Smith was here and she did something. She brought progress to a backward area, refinement to an untamed land, and generosity to a people who didn't know how to give it back in return." And if they put that on my gravestone, I'll die a happy woman.

FREDERICK DOUGLASS
(1818–1895)

Born Frederick Augustus Washington Baily, in Baltimore, Maryland, Douglass was a slave who escaped, changed his name, and went on to become the most articulate and passionate spokesman of the antislavery movement. He was an abolitionist, a newspaper editor, a public speaker of renown, a politician (he once ran for vice president of the United States), and an author. He wrote three autobiographies: *Narrative Life of Frederick Douglass, My Bondage and My Freedom,* and *Life and Times of Frederick Douglass.* In 1877, President Rutherford B. Hayes made him the marshal of the District of Columbia. And in 1889, he was appointed minister and consul general to Haiti. He was also known as an outspoken champion of women's rights.

Frederick Douglass had a long and busy life in which he accomplished so many great things for America and African Americans that I wanted to give a sense of how this extraordinary man developed; hence the view of young Frederick in "Talkin' 'Bout Slavery."

 Talkin' 'Bout Slavery
(a rap)

Young Frederick—Fred—twenty-one, handsome, and muscular, dressed in baggy slacks and an open shirt, talks as he moves around the stage like a contemporary rapper. (There should be some rhythmic beat to accompany his words.)

Fred:

It can't be true, can't be part of God's plan
for one man to be a slave of his fellowman.

I'm just a kid but I know something is wrong
and I can't wait to grow up and to be big and strong.
So I can talk out against it all over the land
and try to make everybody I meet understand
that everyone is equal, that everyone's the same.
And that this thing called slavery is an American shame.

Now I'm gonna tell you something I seen,
and then you can tell me this condition ain't mean.
There was a slave named Barney you ought to know,
who was preparing Colonel Lloyd's horse for some kinda show.
He brushed it and walked it and taught it to obey
so it would do the Colonel proud on the show day.

Now everybody knowed that Barney was the best
a' training a horse and putting it to the test.
It was a gift he had everybody used to say.
A gift from God that made him that way.
He had a reputation that went far and wide.
And in that rep the Colonel took pride.
"My darkie's the best darkie," the Colonel would say.
"And don't any of you other planters try to steal him away."

Now Barney was a friendly and quiet man
who tried to serve his master the best way he can.
"The good Lord made me a slave and I got to obey."
Those were the words Barney always used to say.

Then one day I saw the Colonel call Barney to heel.
And whip him and whip him until the poor man began to squeal.
"What I do, Master, what I do tell me please?"
The Colonel just frowned and said, "Get down on your knees."
When Barney was down he whipped him some more.
He whipped him till Barney's whole body was sore.
He never did tell Barney what he did wrong.
All he said when he was finished was, "Now get along."

He makes a kicking motion.

42

That's the story of slavery in a nutshell.
Every day for a slave is a living hell.
Here's Barney who was beat and didn't know why.
And all he could do was sit in the corner and cry.

A grown man crying is a sad thing to see.
A grown man left without any dignity.
So I swore that day that my life wouldn't be the same,
I would fight against slavery because it's America's shame.

Pause.

I used to work hard every night and every day
and pray for the Lord at night to come take me away.
Other slaves felt the same way that I did
and one man named Dimby ran away and hid.
Where he was going he didn't care
he just wanted to be far, far away from here.
They found him the next day hung from a tree.
I just stood there and watched and said, "God have mercy on me."

Now although I try to behave I was always in trouble.
For speaking out of turn or not moving "on the double."
"We gotta break his spirit," my owner the Colonel said.
"We gotta do it now before someone shoots him dead."
So they brought in a man, Covey was his name.
Slave breaking was his profession, slave managing was his game.

True to his word Covey kept me on the run.
Soon as one job was finished there was another to be done.
I started at four in the morning until twelve at night
then slept for a little and woke up with a fright.
Because there standing above me was Covey with a grin
Saying, "Get up boy, this ain't no hotel you livin' in."

Other slaves used to try to run away and get free.
Covey would hunt them down and beat them unmercifully.
One slave when he couldn't take it no more

jumped in the lake and tried to swim to the other shore.
Covey took his rifle and told the man to stop.
When the man didn't he pulled the trigger, "Pop."
The man's brain exploded and that was the end
of a man that tried to be everybody's friend.

Pause.

I was sixteen years old but I felt like I was forty-five.
Every day became a burden of trying to stay alive.
I just wanted it to stop and I was really trying to behave
because all I wanted now was to be an ordinary slave.
Now every man has a limit past which we shouldn't dare.
But if Covey knew it he just didn't seem to care.
I was going to be the star in his crown
so he didn't care how much he beat me down.

Now common sense tells us that even a dog will rebel
if you push him too hard or make his life hell.
So one day I stood up to Covey simple and plain
and said, "You can yell at me, Mr. Covey, but you ain't hittin' me again."
He came at me fast and I got outta the way
but I had to be careful because the state laws did say
that if a slave struck a white man he could be hung that very same day.
We circled each other while Covey tried with his whip
to get me in his grip.
"You better kill me," I yelled, "because I'm tellin' you now
if you raise your hand to me I'm gonna break it off some how."
He made a leap for me and I grabbed him in a clinch
and held on to him so tight he couldn't budge an inch.
He twisted and stamped and even tried to bite,
but I had him in my grip and I had him real tight.
We struggled and struggled all over the place
with him fighting hard to save himself from grace.
But I was so strong and determined that day
that nothing he tried could move me in any way.

We wrestled and wrestled for an hour, then two,

and he got so frustrated that he didn't know what to do.
I wasn't hitting him, I was just holding him strong
and I intended to hold him like that all day long.
Or until the Colonel would come to break it up.
Now Covey didn't want the Colonel to see him losing to this pup.
So I let him go. Like a wet dog or duck
he slinked out of the yard as the other slaves watched.

Nobody whistled or cheered even though they wanted to.
We were all happy that the contest was over and the battle was
   through.
And as they went back to their chores they all raised their fist for
   me to see
that what I had scored was a quiet moral victory.

I'm talking about slavery a real bad condition
and it used to be a part of the American tradition.

◉ I Will Raise Both My Hands ◉

Frederick Douglass, in his fifties, stands at a podium dressed in period garb.

Frederick:

There is a story about two poisonous snakes. One's facing the north, the other facing south. One's name is Freedom, the other, Slavery. Both bit the Negro and both bites were bad. . . . The Civil War was over but our battle had just begun.

No sooner had the war ended than the Southern states began enacting "black codes" and "penal laws" to return the freed slaves to the control of their former masters. Mississippi prohibited black men from owning or even renting land. South Carolina and other states were forcing black women to work as hired farm hands or domestics for cruelly low wages or face arrest as vagrants. The employers had the power to starve black people to death and that, to my mind, was still the power of slavery. Under these conditions, what does freedom mean?

I thought about it, then thought about it some more. And although officially retired, I had to speak my piece.

Moves to center stage.

Slavery is not abolished until the black man has the ballot. While the legislature of the South retains the right to pass laws making any discrimination between black and white, slavery still lives there.

If the Negro knows enough to fight for his country, he knows enough to vote. If he knows enough to pay taxes, he knows enough to vote. The government thinks it's done enough for the slaves by freeing them, but this freed slave is still a slave to society. If a man can't vote or exercise his rights as a citizen, what's the purpose of his being free in a democracy? If the black man is to have any hope of surviving, he must be given the ballot now.

The sound of applause as Douglass goes back to his desk.

As I traveled the country agitating for the vote, opposition came from a very curious place. Here is a letter I received from Elizabeth Cady Stanton:

> Dear Mr. Douglass,
>
> The representative women of this nation have done their utmost for the last thirty years to secure freedom for the Negro. Now that this has been achieved, what about women's rights? The old antislavery school says that women must stand back until the rights of Negroes are recognized. But on this question of suffrage I say, if you will not give the whole load to the entire people, then give it to the most intelligent first. Women.

I could not agree and told her so. I explained that the cause of Negro suffrage was more urgent to me, because Negroes were being lynched, shot, castrated, and burned at the stake. We needed the vote for our protection.

When women, because they are women, are dragged from their homes and hung upon lampposts, and when their children are torn from their arms, then they will have the urgency to obtain the ballot ahead of the black man.

We battled this issue in public and in private. And this battle was especially painful to me because it put me at odds with so many women whom I had respected and admired. Women like Harriet Beecher Stowe, Elizabeth Cady Stanton, and Susan B. Anthony. But I could not be stopped and would not be stopped. There was too much at stake for the black man at this juncture. And then finally, finally it came to pass.

He reads from a document.

Fourteenth Amendment

No state shall make or enforce any law which shall abridge the privileges or immunities of citizens of the United States; nor shall any state deprive any person of life, liberty, or property, without due process of law; nor deny any person within its jurisdiction the equal protection of the laws. Ratified July 28, 1868.

He reads from another document.

Fifteenth Amendment
The right of citizens of the United States to vote shall not be denied or abridged by the United States or by any state on account of race, color, or previous condition of servitude. Ratified March 30, 1870.

The battle, on paper at least, was won. But how expensive was the cost? I wondered if I could now reach out the arm of friendship and be thus embraced by those who through necessities of their own had been made opponents to our cause.

He rises.

I am happy to say, I could. And I was once again invited to the platforms where women's rights were being championed.

He moves to center stage.

Man in his arrogance has hitherto felt himself fully equal to the work of governing without the help of women. He has kept the reins of power securely in his own hands, and the history of nations and the present experience of the world show the woeful work he has made of governing.

The slaveholders used to represent the salves, the rich landowners in other countries represent the poor, and the men in our country claim to represent women. But the true doctrine of American liberty plainly is that each class and each individual of a class should be allowed to represent themselves.

The right of women to vote is sacred in my judgment. And if called upon to give my assent in any official capacity, I will raise both my hands in favor. And this is a right that should be given as quickly as possible.

Slavery of one kind has ended, but another continues. So long as women are refused the right to vote, they are enslaved. Therefore, I urge you to petition your congressmen and representatives on this important subject. For the sooner women are allowed to vote, the sooner America will truly be the land of the free.

Are we free, I wonder. Will we ever be truly free? Or is freedom an abstraction that can never be made into a practical reality? I sometimes think I know. But often times I'm baffled. Yet of this much I'm sure. Freedom, whether an abstraction or fact, is something worth fighting for. So the battle continues.

Lights fade slowly as he goes back to his writing.

"GENERAL" BUDDOE
(1820–?)

Slavery in the Virgin Islands, then under Danish rule, ended some fifteen years before the end of slavery in the United States. On July 2, 1848, at a prearranged hour, all the slaves on the island of St. Croix, some three thousand in number, left their various estates, took up whatever arms they could find (machetes, clubs, spears, torches, etc.), and marched into the town of Christiansted, terrifying the white Danish inhabitants by demanding their freedom. On being told that the governor (Von Scholten), who was absent at the time, was the only one in authority who could grant their request, the slaves went on a rampage, smashing and burning a number of government buildings and offices, but did not touch private residents. The following day when Governor Von Scholten, who was known to be sympathetic to the plight of the slaves, did arrive, he listened to the slaves' demands and sequestered himself for awhile. After several hours he returned with a signed proclamation that freed all the slaves.

Local legend has it that the architect of this uprising and the demand for unconditional freedom was an educated slave who called himself General Buddoe. He was a charismatic and enigmatic leader who it was said visited with Governor Von Scholten and convinced him to sign the emancipation proclamation. What became of Buddoe is unknown. The rumor is that he left the island the following day and was never heard from again.

We Will Ask, But We Won't Beg

"General" Buddoe, age twenty-eight, tall, well-spoken, dressed in a colorful military jacket and a hat, is talking to a group of slaves on the street at night.

Buddoe:

Listen to me. Settle down a while please and listen to me. There's something I have to say. Something happened tonight, something new, and we have to pay attention to it and think about what it means. What it seriously means. Because the outcome of what we do now could mean the end of our situation as slaves, starting at this moment. Starting tonight.

Pause.

When we left our estates today, it was to send the king of Denmark a message. And to tell the citizens of Denmark living here on this island that they had better start to think fast about the situation of slavery. And start to think about making some changes in their lives, because we are planning to make some changes in ours. What we're trying to tell them in our own way is that they better learn to work. They better learn to ride mules, carry rocks, cut sugarcane, and catch fish. Or they better learn to pay a living wage to the people on this island if they want us to work for them any more. Because there is not going to be any such thing as working for free anymore. Because they ain't gonna be any such thing as slaves, or "unfree" as these Danish people like to call us.

They tell us to wait twelve years for freedom, and we tell them it's too long. They tell us to wait, and we tell them we are sick and tired of waiting. They tell us to be peaceful, and we tell them to go to hell. We been peaceful long enough.

Tonight we were going to show them just a small show of our force, but already things have gone much beyond that. We showed them our numbers, and frightened them too much. Burn things too much, threaten them too much. So the way it stand is if we don't get what we set out for this night, we will lose everything we gained in the last several years. Because this white man, if he can subdue us, will not give us more, he will just take it all away from us. So it's a win or lose situation. We either lose it all or get it all.

Pause.

Remember when the decree was read and nailed to the trees telling us that all children of slaves would be free? But we the parents and friends would have to wait for twelve years before we could be like our children. (*He reads from the decree*) Here's what it says: "The law but royal decree states that all children hereafter born to slaves are born free. And the present slaves will be declared free in twelve years. Or more properly the year of our Lord 1859." What did they think would happen? How did they think we would feel? Did they think that we were going to get on our knees and say thank you? Well if they did, they were wrong. Are we supposed to forget how these people changed our fathers and mothers from human to animal just by working them so long in the sun? And we were the ones to watch their eyes turn red and blind. And their skin turn to leather like that of a cow just from being out in the sun too long. And their body bent and broken from bending over and carrying too much weight. That's what they want for our future, and that's what another twelve years will do to us. We want our freedom, and we want it now.

If force is necessary, I am ready to fight. I am ready to die. I am ready to fight and die rather than be a slave for one more day. And I know that is true of all of you too. And I want to say to the king of Denmark, tell him how we feel, so he knows what he has to do. What he better do. The problem is the king isn't here. The king is a million miles away in Denmark. But I heard something today. I got to talking to a man in the Danish government. This is a man who should know. And what he said to me was that the king doesn't have to sign any papers setting us free. The governor of this island, Governor Von Scholten, he can sign the decree in the name of the king and the king has to honor it. This man swears to me that it is true. Now I don't know if he was telling me a story just to save his own neck, but I'm going to find out. I intend to find out tonight.

You see, we have them going tonight but in the long run, especially if they get help from Puerto Rico or other places, we can't beat them. We can't beat them with words, and we can't beat them with weapons if they get really organized. What we have right now is the numbers and the will. The will to be free men.

So this is my plan. I plan to visit with the governor and explain in a quiet way what we need him to do. I plan to try to deal and negotiate. I plan to show him respect, but tell him how we feel and how determined we are. The governor has already shown that he is a fair man by all that he has already done on our behalf. No other governor has done as much to improve and change our condition. Now it's time for him to take the next step. What I plan to try and make him understand is that the taste for our freedom is in the air and it won't go away. The time is now for him to take the next step that will make history for this island.

But if he doesn't do it, what we've started now on this night is just the beginning of what's to come in days ahead. It's all in his hands. Quiet and peace, or blood and destruction from one end of this island to the next. All he has to do is sign the decree and put his seal on it and it will stop what's going on in the streets right now. And the kind of slaughter that people will probably be talking about and writing about a hundred years from now. Like I said to you before, I will ask, but I won't beg.

I think the governor will understand, and I think he will hear what we have to say. Let us hope to God and seize the light and not let it get to the point when the sun rises tomorrow that this whole island has become a graveyard of bodies and souls. That's what I plan to say to the governor and let's hope he has the wisdom to listen and do what is right.

HARRIET TUBMAN
(1821–1913)

Harriet Tubman was born in Dorchester, Maryland. She was the daughter of two slaves who were not legally permitted to marry under the laws of slavery. As a child Harriet was thought to be stupid and was treated harshly. But she survived the treatment and became a hardworking field hand. At age twenty-five, Harriet, with her two brothers, planned an escape to the North and freedom. On the way, her brothers became discouraged and turned back, but Harriet continued.

After her successful escape, she became a "conductor" for the Underground Railroad movement. She made nineteen trips back to the South and led three hundred slaves out of bondage. Her success was such that there was a forty-thousand-dollar bounty on her head. But she was never caught.

During the Civil War, she worked as a cook, a scout, a nurse, and a spy. After the war, she established a home for needy blacks, who were wandering the country with no place to go. Tubman, who was called the Moses of her people, died in 1913. Today she's one of the most honored and revered African American women in history.

Mr. John Brown and Me

Harriet Tubman, age thirty-eight, is talking to a group of ex-slaves in Canada.

Harriet:

I is a praying woman, and I gon' continue to be a praying woman till the end of my days. But sometimes, sometimes I gotta ask if the Lord God know what he doin' when he do things in a certain way. Or maybe he just fall asleep and just wasn't payin' no attention.

Because they got to be a reason why a blessed man in a righteous cause didn't get to carry out his holy plan to rid the world of evil so's goodness can prevail.

John Brown was a righteous man, no doubt about that. But now everybody callin' him the devil and sayin' that anybody that follow him was spawn from hell too. But to me the ones who sayin' that, them be the devil. Them be the ones spawn from Satan fires. I know this to be true, because I knowed Mr. Brown and I know the system he was fighting. I know the system good, because that's the same system that I been fightin' too. Been fightin' it since I heard the Bible story a Moses leading the Israelites outta Egypt across the Red Sea.

I been fightin' it ever since Mr. Brodas hired me to that Bucktown owner, and he throw that scale weight to hit that runaway who was hiding in a store. I didn't know who that boy was, but I seen his eyes for a quick bit. He was over there, shopkeeper Evans was over here behind the counter, and I was by the door. When he see the boy, shopkeeper shout for me to stop him since the boy was runnin' for the door. And that's when I see his eyes all crazy and wild and begging for help. I didn't know what to do. I didn't want a beating for not obeying, but I didn't want to be helping Mr. Evans, who was as mean as a skunk when he feel like it. So I just act like I didn't understand what he was sayin' to me. You see, peoples always callin' me stupid, so it wasn't nothin' for me to act like it was true. So I just act like I didn't understand what Mr. Evans was sayin'. I just rub my head and say kinda slow, "Yes sir, what you want, sir?" And while I was sayin' that I was kinda edging out of the doorway so's the runaway could get clear. He couldn't a been more'n a year or so older than me. And I was fifteen at the time.

"Stop him I say!" Massa Evans call out again, and again I still make like I wasn't hearing him too good. And that's when Massa Evans take up that iron scale weight and throw it at the boy. Only thing is his throw was bad. I kinda still remember it coming at me, but I couldn't get outta the way fast enough. That weight hit me and I was gone. When I wake up again, late that night, Mamma was rubbing a wet cloth on my head. The first thing I ask was if that boy had got away. When she said yes, in spite of all the pain I was feelin' I could feel myself smile. The knock on my head a done some good. And to this day I still get pains from that knock. And sometimes I even fall down and get visions while's I is fallin'. The pain from that knock gon' probably follow me all my life, however long that gon' be. But I'll always remember that in spite of the pain, it done somebody some good.

Pause.

I met up with Mr. John Brown two years ago. He had heared about me and the work I been doin' to help slaves get free. And he told some people that he wanted to meet up and talk with me. I was so proud to hear that. I had knowed about Mr. Brown and what he was doin' for our people, and it made me feel special that a man so great would want to meet and talk with me.

Pause.

From the moment I meet him and he shake my hand, I knowed that he was a special man, a man apart from all the rest. First there was his eyes, big, wide, and steady. He look at you and you could tell he wasn't just lookin' at your face but at your soul as well. And that he was seein' every dark corner and every bright spot in it too.

Then there was his voice. Deep, brown, and rolling. Rolling like thunder coming down from the mountains. And before I could say much, he say to me that he had a vision that I was destined to be America's Joan of Arc. "It came to me in a dream," he said. Then he called me General Harriet, and told me that I was the bravest woman in America today. "We were put on this continent and in this place at the same time for a reason. You and me we were put here to fight and win a holy war. A war that will free this country of the most rampant evil on this earth: slavery."

"Amen," I had to say to that. And then he started to tell me about his plan for Harpers Ferry. How the weapons he would be gettin' there would give the slaves equal footing in the field of battle.

"This country can be a great country," he said. "But a great country cannot be built on a foundation of evil. That's why we must fight this war. That's why we must take these weapons and create an army made of slaves. We will start small, but in time multitudes and multitudes of slaves will join us. We will become a force. We will become a tidal wave. And no army on earth will be able to stop us, until we have finished what we have started to do. And when we are through, this country and maybe the world will be cleansed of this evil like the way it was cleansed by the flood after Noah."

As I listened to him, I was hypnotize where I was standing. It was like I was listening to John the Baptist telling of the coming of Our Lord Jesus Christ.

"I want to know that I can call on you when the time comes. I need your talent, I need your brain, and I need your experience."

I told him that he could count on me. That I would be ready whenever he would need me.

"We are in a holy war," he said. "A war for a righteous cause. And we are going to win this war and win it for one big reason. God is on our side."

Pause.

Well it wasn't till two years later that Mr. Brown called for me. And I was ready and willing to go. But as things would have it, the falling-down blackness from that blow on my head years ago took me over. And when I wake up I was feverish and weak. I try to get up, try to move around, but the sickness and fever wouldn't let me. I was so weak I couldn't even think hard enough to pray for Mr. Brown to be successful. I would start to pray and my eyes would close and I would fall asleep again. This situation with me lasted for nearly a week. But I knowed with or without me Mr. Brown and his men were going to do what they set out to do.

When I was myself again, I heard the news that Mr. Brown and his men went on the raid, and how they had been shot up and kill, most of them. And how Mr. Brown hisself had been wounded and then hanged out in the public for everybody to see. I cried when I heard that, and I ask my Lord in heaven, "Why?"

Then after a while it come to me. The Lord had one plan for Mr. Brown and he had another for me. If I had been well and had make the trip, I woulda been either shot or hung with all the rest of them. So the Lord make me sick so I had to stay here and not be part of the massacre. You see, I have a different job. I can see that now, my job is to carry on. John Brown had his job, I got mine. John Brown was a man and a hero. He wasn't crazy like everybody say he was. He was blessed, and he did his part. Now it's up to us to do ours.

HATTIE MCDANIEL
(1895–1953)

Hattie McDaniel was the first African American (male or female) to win the coveted Academy Award for acting. She was voted best supporting actress, for *Gone with the Wind,* in 1939. Ms. McDaniel began her career as a professional band singer. She was also a talented actress, and won her first acting award when she was fifteen. In 1932, she played her first motion picture role, and she continued working right into the 1950s, when she died of cancer.

Although she was a well-trained and versatile actress, McDaniel was mostly cast as a maid or the eternal "black mammy." This image was a blessing and a curse; on one hand it kept her constantly employed, and on the other hand it stereotyped her in the eyes of many, particularly African Americans, who found the image demeaning. But if one looks closely at her many film performances, one sees that she frequently transcended the stereotypes through wit, sly attitudes, and a great deal of humor.

Nobody Knows and Yet They Talk

Hattie, age fifty, is sitting comfortably in her living room, talking to a friend who also happens to be a reporter.

Hattie:

You know I done live long enough to know that the world is all about contradictions. To know that most people is all about making noise about things they know nothing about. All you gotta do is read the newspapers or listen to the radio. This one contradicting that one, while the other is sayin' that the next one don't know what he's talking about and so on and so on. Especially here in Hollywood where everything you see or hear is made up. They make up your hair, your face, the clothes you wear in front of the camera, and the clothes you wear when you go out in public. They make up the stories and the people that they show in the movies. You the performer play the part, yes, but they is the one make up the character that you have to play. And there nothin' you can do about it. Oh yeah, you can touch it up here and there, add a little somethin' sometimes like the spice you put in a pot of gumbo. And sometimes if you lucky, they might ask your opinion on how such and such a person would talk and act if they feel that them who write the scripts ain't got it right. But in the end, all the main ingredients is the stuff that they put in.

So, what I guess I'm sayin' is you can't blame the performer for the parts they play. Still people do it all the time. People confuse what they see up on screen for what they think is happening in real life and forget that it's all make-believe. Fairy tales and lies to entertain people and make them spend a lot of money.

Now, for the most part I don't listen to criticism or pay much attention to what people say I do or don't do. First of all, I know my job. My job is acting in the movies, and I been doin' it for a whole lotta years now. So nobody can say I don't know what I'm doing, because I've had a whole lotta experience. I'm an experienced professional.

I made my first moving picture in 1932, and since that time I've been going from one picture to another. Sometimes it seems I been going without stopping to catch my breath. In 1936, for example, I made eleven motion pictures. In 1937 I was in seven. And all them was full-blown parts. Tell me somebody else, colored or white, in this business that can match that record. So don't tell me that I don't know what I'm about, because I damn well do and that's a fact.

Now everybody knows that Hollywood is the kind of place it is. People work, people make money. A whole lotta money. People dress up, go out wave and smile for the camera. Then go back home and hide till the next time they have to do it. But what most people don't know is that almost everybody in Hollywood is running scared. Especially the producers and them studio bosses. Oh, they might act bossy and try to push people around to show how powerful they is and how tough they can be. But when you move all that aside, them people is running scared. More scared than you and me, for one simple reason. They got more on the table, so they got more to lose.

Take a man as big-time and as powerful as David O. He got more money than any of us can imagine, and more power than most of us want in a lifetime. But still he running scared too.

When he hired me for *Gone with the Wind,* know what he said to me? He said, "Hattie, I want you to play the part with all the power and strength you can muster. I want this woman to be independent, forceful, and strong. She might be a slave, but she is her own woman too. I want that in the performance, and I'm going to instruct the writers to write it that way so you'll have something solid to work from."

I told him, "I appreciate that."

"I want all the colored parts in this picture to have strength and dignity," he said. "I want the colored people of this country to feel proud of who they are when they see this film. The colored press and the NAACP can be very hard on the motion pictures when they want to. I want them to see that things are different with a Selznick picture. You see, what most people in this industry don't understand or sometimes even admit to is that the colored population contributes a sizeable percent to the box office receipts of most motion pictures. And for this one I want every colored person in this country to come and see it when we have it showing in the theatres."

And he kept his word. David O. was no liar, I'll say that for him. All through the months and years that it took to shoot that picture, no matter how busy he was with other things. And believe me when I tell you there was lots of stuff to keep that man busy day and night. Still, in spite of all that busyness he always take the time to talk to me and Thelma [*Butterfly McQueen*] and Oscar [*Polk*] about our parts and how we felt about what we was doin'.

Now the role of Mammy was something I was after right from the beginning. I had been told about the book and that Mr. Selznick was going to make a motion picture out of it. And it was going to be a big picture. *The biggest motion picture in the history*, is what his studio was sayin' about this one. So, I went out, got the book, and read it. Right away I knew the role I wanted to play; I don't know why, I just did. I had the sense that I could do the right thing by it. And since I'd been in so many movies, I knew they had to consider me. They said I had to take a test, and I said sure. They tested me and some other women and then asked me to come by and test again. It wasn't till after the third test that they said I had the part.

It was like a dream come true. Then the dream started turning a little bit into a nightmare. We had so many directors, so much fighting with the creative people, so many changes and rewrites, that day to day none of us knew if any of it was going to make any sense. After a while it just looked like this film was never going to get finished. That David O. would run out of money and the whole thing would just be a bust. People in the business was already calling it Selznick's Folly, and some was even taking bets that it was going to break him for sure. I remember even Clark [*Gable*] saying, "I wonder if this thing's ever going to be finished, or are we all going to just grow old, wither up, and die while this eternal shoot goes on."

The only one that didn't seem to have any doubts about the picture was David O. He was like St. George fighting one dragon at a time, beating him down and then going on to the next one. When the film was finally finished, we all breathed a big sigh of relief, I know I did. I had given that picture everything I had and now I was exhausted.

When it was finally put together, the music and titles, and all the war scenes was cut in, there was a private screening at MGM and we was all invited to come over and see it. I watched the whole thing; I got to say it took my breath away. The big opening premiere was in Atlanta, and I started making plans about what I was going to wear. Then came the word, I wasn't invited. None of the colored people in the picture was invited to the big opening. This wasn't David O.'s idea. This order came from the mayor and the good white Christian citizens of Atlanta. They didn't want anything colored at that premiere. They even asked to have my picture taken off the back of the movie program. And they did. But they had to rush a last-minute printing to get it ready for that night, and somehow they managed it. Now you gotta understand David O. coulda said no. He coulda moved the premiere someplace else like New York or L.A., but he didn't. He obeyed those people's orders about keeping us out. That's what I mean about runnin' scared. His was afraid of the backlash he might get in the South concerning the picture if he had let us come. So what I'm sayin' is he was runnin' scared of them, although he probably wouldn't admit it even if you put a gun to his head.

The big-time critics that wrote about the picture wasn't afraid of them bigots. They wrote about how fine a picture it was and how wonderful Vivien and Clark was. Especially Vivien. And then they went on to say, "Hattie McDaniel is a force of nature in this giant of a motion picture. And if Hollywood doesn't recognize her contribution at awards time, then we all have to ask what are the awards really about?"

Well as you know, Olivia [*De Havilland*] and me was nominated for best supporting actress. And when they called my name out as the winner, all the people at the dinner stood up and gave me a standing ovation. I went up to the stage, and gave a speech that David O. had made the writers write for me. "This award is very important," he said, "and the possibility of you winning it is very real. If you do, it would be a big step forward for all the actors in our industry. And a big boost for all the colored as well, so you want to be careful with what you say. You want it to be phrased just right." And that's how it come to be that a bunch of white men who didn't know squat about me got to write the thank-you speech that I had to deliver. But that didn't bother me none. Any more than the fact that although I was a nominee I didn't get to sit at the main dinner table at the Coconut Grove with all the other nominees. Me and my date had to sit at a side table in the corner of the restaurant. But like I said that didn't matter none. I had won, that was all that was important. I said the stupid speech. It wasn't really stupid. It was harmless, that's what it was, harmless. And it wasn't what I would have said if I had had my way. But I didn't care, I had won.

At the end of the speech I broke down and cried, because at that moment I was remembering all the mountains I had to climb over and all the rivers I had to cross to get to this place. I had a lifetime of ups and downs for five or maybe seven minutes in the spotlight. And you find yourself asking, "Was it all worth it?" You bet your behind it was worth it. *Hattie McDaniel, the thirteenth child of a Baptist minister, born in Wichita, Kansas, singer of gospel songs and the blues, who was billed as everything from the colored Sophie Tucker and the female Bert William to Hi-Hat-Hattie. Came to Hollywood as a maid, in the ladies room of a nightclub . . . and now the first black person to win motion pictures' highest award for acting.* That wasn't just a golden moment, that was history. And there ain't nothin' anybody can do to change that.

But with every success come criticism. And the most hurtful for me was when my own started to attack me for playing maids and domestics. Sayin' that I was keepin' the race down and makin' us look like a nation of servants to the rest of the world. The problem is they have no idea of what it's like out here. Still, they go on the radio and write in newspapers that I'm belittlin' the race with the parts I play. They act like Eddie Anderson, Thelma McQueen, or me could walk into Twentieth Century–Fox, Paramount, or MGM and tell them what we want and don't want. Can't nobody do that. Not even Clark Gable or Spencer Tracy. You do that and you don't work, it's as simple as that. Yet these people who don't know nothin' about this jumpin' up and criticizing me. But like I always say, and I know what I'm talkin' about, 'cause I been in both places, "It's better to earn seven thousand dollars a week playing a maid than be one for seven dollars a week."

If people want to talk and criticize, they should know what it is they are talkin' about. Me and all the other colored folks out here acting in movies are performers, not politicians. We tryin' to make a living like everybody else. When we can, we try to change a line or the style of a character in a script when they look like they tryin' to make fools of us. But most of time we have to do it through acting in a way that the director or producer don't notice; sometime it's through a look or an attitude that we are sayin' this character or that person we playin' ain't just some lowdown individual. That this is an intelligent human being put in that position. But we have to do it in character, that's the hard part. Because if we don't, that would be bad acting. That's how it is for us.

So I ain't ashamed of what I do, or how I act up there on the screen. I am a professional, and I have this award to prove it. To them people who want to criticize there ain't nothin' I can do or say that can change their minds. They can just go on criticizing, and I can just go on doing what I've been doing all these years. And who knows, there may be even more awards in the future.

JACKIE ROBINSON
(1919–1972)

Born in Cairo, Georgia, Jackie Robinson was educated at UCLA, where he excelled in football, basketball, baseball, and track. After some time spent in the U.S. Army, Robinson decided to play professional baseball with the Negro American League. In 1945, he was signed by the Brooklyn Dodgers organization and apprenticed in the minor league. In 1947, he joined the Dodgers and became the first black person to play major league baseball. That year he was named Rookie of the Year. In 1949, he was Most Valuable Player of the Year. In his overall career he compiled a batting average of .311, played in six winning pennants and one World Series Championship. He retired after the 1956 season and was named to the Baseball Hall of Fame in 1962. After retirement he became a business executive and spokesman as well as a fundraiser for the civil rights movement.

Jackie Robinson, while on vacation in St. Thomas, Virgin Islands, came to the school I attended and spoke to our class, signing autographs for all of us. In this monologue, I've tried to produce much of what he said as well as I remember it.

Baseball and Character

Jackie Robinson, age thirty-five, is sitting on a desk in a classroom, talking to some eighth graders.

Jackie:

Hey, everybody, how you all this morning? (*Waits for a response*) Good. You all look so bright and shiny, just like that new dime I found yesterday. It was shining so bright saying, "Pick me up . . . pick me up." So that's what I did. Picked it up and put it into my pocket. Hope it brings me luck.

Your teacher said you all like baseball. Said you got a couple of teams going. And that you're all great baseball fans. Said that I should talk to you about my life and about the game and maybe give you a few pointers on how to hold your bat or pitch. So we'll do all that. It'll be my pleasure. (*Hears a question from the back*) Yes? . . . What am I doing here? Why am I not back in Brooklyn with my team? Well you see, the season is over, as you know. We won the World Series so we are taking some time off. The celebrating is over and now it's our time to get some rest and start thinking about the next season. My way of relaxing is to play golf. I love the game, although I can't play it well. And you got a great golf course here. Everyone said I should play it, so that's what I'm doing, playing on your golf course. But don't worry I'll be back in Brooklyn soon. And I won't forget to say hello to all the other guys for you, and tell them what great ball fans you are.

Your teacher said I should talk a little bit about myself, so we'll so that. My name is Jack Roosevelt Robinson, as you know. I play ball for the Brooklyn Dodgers and I love the game. I love everything about it, the batting, the fielding, the fans, and the complications it can put you through. Complications that make you have to use your body, your mind, and your ingenuity too. See, you have to figure out how to read your opposing player and figure out what he's trying to do before he does it. And then figure out what you're gonna do when he does. This all works in a flash of a second sometimes, and the only clue you have is maybe the look in his eye or the way he turns his head or the way he bends his shoulders. Body language is what they call it. You learn to read the other team's body language and hope you're right about what you're reading. Then you play off that. That's what I mean by ingenuity.

Now baseball is not about a single individual, it's about a team of people working together to achieve one goal: winning the game. After that, winning a whole lotta games. And when you add them all together, winning the Pennant, and then winning the World Series. Teamwork. Everybody playing their positions, doing what they do best. But most of all it's about backing each other up. Being there when your teammate needs you. And knowing that he'll be there whenever you need him. In this game teamwork is everything. Without it you'll never get anywhere. And that's true in life too. I don't care who you are, how much money you have or how much power, we all need each other, and we always will.

But baseball is about character too. It's about being honest and strong and never afraid. Everybody likes to write about the fact that I'm the first black player to play major league baseball. And that is true. There're more black players in the game now, but I was the first. And that was not all that long ago, in 1947. When it was first announced, there was a lot of bad reactions from people who love to make noise more than listen to common sense. People who love their own hate more than they could ever love the game. But it was done because the time was right. Somebody had to break that color barrier and that somebody turned out to be me. Coulda been a hundred other guys who's just as good and just as talented. But they happened to choose me. Or should I say one man chose me. A man with the strength and honesty and courage I was talking about. That man was Branch Rickey, the general manager of our team. He looked at me play and saw something he liked. That's what the general managers do. They scout around for players they think could fit into their teams and make a solid contribution. At the time I was playing second base for the Montreal Royals and that was a nice job to have, but it wasn't major leagues. Before that I had been playing with the Kansas City Monarchs of the Negro American League. But my real beginnings was at UCLA, where I ran track and played football and basketball before discovering how much I loved baseball. So you see, it's good to try a lot of sports out just to find the one for you. It's kind of letting the game or the sport pick you out instead of the other way around.

Now, when I latched on to baseball I wouldn't let it go. I practiced every chance I had between the jobs I had and the lessons I had to study. I read up all I could about the history of the game. And about our history in it. I found out, for example, that it was colored soldiers in the Union Army during the Civil War looking at white soldiers playing the game that decided to try it out themselves. That in 1885 a man named Frank Thompson organized the first Negro team that paid its members to play. He called them the Cuban

Giants, so that they could play in the South. And they had to pretend to speak Spanish in order not to have race troubles, but that's where it began. After that we been playing the game regularly for over fifty years now.

When I came along and Mr. Rickey signed me to the team, everybody said it would ruin the game. I didn't know what they meant. All I wanted to do was play ball to the best of my ability. I wanted to play with the best team because I knew that would challenge me and make me a better player. I didn't have any prejudice against white players, so I didn't think they would have any against me. And most of them didn't. But it was Mr. Rickey that did it all. He said to me, "Jackie, there's gonna be a lotta noise, and a lotta opposition to this. But they're wrong and I'm right. So just ignore it if you can, and play the best ball you capable of. That's all I want from everybody in my team, their best."

The other players welcomed me and made me feel at home. I'll always be grateful for that. Because without their support I don't know how I would of gotten through that first season. But still, I have to go back to Branch and say that he was the man with the courage and foresight to say that it was time. And that it was going to happen.

Baseball is a wonderful sport. An American sport. A man can hit a ball harder and farther than anybody else. A man can run and steal more bases quicker and faster. A man can throw and catch better, and all that is nice, all that is exciting and thrilling. But when a man stands up against the world for what he believes, puts his heart and future out there for that same belief, that man is a giant. That man is bigger than the game. And to me Mr. Branch Rickey is that person. And they don't come any bigger.

Now I'll take questions. You can ask me anything, and I'll try to answer as best I can.

JAMES BALDWIN
(1924–1987)

James Baldwin was a writer in the fullest sense of the word. He wrote novels, poems, plays, screenplays, essays, and a children's book. He was and still is regarded as one of the best writers America has produced in the latter half of the twentieth century. Best known for his essays, James Baldwin became the window through which white America could view the fire and the passion of the black man's soul.

I met James Baldwin in 1985, at Virginia Commonwealth University, right after I had adapted his novel, Go Tell It on the Mountain, *for a PBS TV movie. He was pleased with the adaptation and with the end result. He was on a lecture tour. We appeared on stage together, had lunch and drinks together, and talked. We discussed the possibility of my adapting some of his other works for the media, but this never came to pass. When he died, it was said that we will never see his like again. His work endures, but his literary fire is still missed.*

 A Dream of Deliverance
(a dual monologue)

When the lights come up, Baldwin, age thirty-eight, is standing behind a podium with notes in front of him. Behind him, one on either side of the stage, stand a man and a woman who serve as a chorus and speak in unison.

Chorus:

James Baldwin . . . American writer, essayist, novelist, playwright, short-story writer, poet, author of children's stories, and civil rights, human rights activist.

He started out in Harlem but ended up in France.

He began his life with gospel but moved on to the blues.

He urged us to *Go Tell It on the Mountain* about *The Fire Next Time*.

Stood at *The Amen Corner* and told us about *Blues for Mr. Charlie*.

Asked *How Long the Train's Been Gone* and talked about *The Price of the Ticket*.

He said the American Negro is really a part of this country. And the day that we face this fact, that's the day we will become a nation. Maybe even a great one.

Baldwin:

I was asked to come here to speak and the subject of course is to be my life. My life as it relates to my writing. But to talk about my writing, I must talk about America. And to talk about America I must talk about race and race relations. How it has stunted and crippled this great nation. And how it will go on crippling us until we come to our senses. Sometime ago I said the American black person is a part of this country, and the day we face up to the fact is the day we become a nation. Maybe even a great one.

I believed it then and despite evidence to the contrary I believe it now. You see, I was born in the church. Gospel, prayers, and optimism have always been a part of my psychic condition. So I am hopeful about America and dream of its deliverance.

Chorus:

On July 29, 1943, his father died. On the same day a few hours later, his father's last child was born.

James was always disturbed by the memory of his father. They did not get along very well. That is an understatement; the truth is they got along very badly. He said, "My father was chilling on the pulpit and incredibly cruel in his personal life. He was the most bitter man I ever met."

But he didn't blame his father. Not wholly anyway. He blamed the conditions in America in helping to shape his father's character.

Conditions that had a big hand in shaping James's character as well.

That's why he thought it ironic that a few hours after his father's funeral, while the old man lay in state at the undertaker's chapel, a riot broke out in Harlem. A race riot.

Baldwin:

All these portents, omens, and signs I took to be a signal to the world that one era had passed and another was just beginning.

I can still see my father. I can still hear his voice. I can still feel his crushing charm. But most of all I can still feel his blackness. He was the blackest man I ever knew and also the proudest.

I thought of being a minister but went off in other directions. Still in my mind the question was never settled. I always had this idea that one day I would wind up going back to the church.

Sometimes at night when I was alone images used to haunt me. They would haunt me all the time. The most terrifying one was the image of my father sitting in a room all by himself, locked in with his anger, his bitterness, and his fear. He would be there all alone for the longest while and then when I looked in the other corner of the room I'd be there with him.

"Son," he would say.

"Father," I would say.

And for the longest while we would talk to each other back and forth, exchanging ideas, opinions, and even jokes. And finally I would say, "Dad why didn't we talk like this before? Why did we have to wait so long?"

But he couldn't hear me. Or maybe he didn't want to hear, because he never gave me an answer. He just sat there in the darkness, staring into space, maintaining his silence forever.

When I was nine going on ten I wrote a play that was directed by a white teacher. This nice lady took an interest in me. She gave me books to read and encouraged me to think about writing. Later on I wrote an essay that won a prize in a citywide essay contest. I even got a letter from the mayor of New York signed personally by him.

My path to being a writer began. But America began to crowd in on me, so I went to Europe and stayed mostly in France. When I returned to America I was a published writer.

I wish my father could have seen my success. I also wish that he had a better life. I think it was at his funeral that I started having that dream. The dream of social harmony that would allow us to hold on to things that matter. And make us reject or ignore things that don't matter. For example, hatred doesn't matter and neither does bitterness. Blackness and whiteness does not matter either. But the dead matter, though, because they live on in our memories. Also the idea of a new life matters, one that will not continue the bad habits of the past.

I was born in Harlem but ended up in France. I started out with gospel but moved on to the blues.

American history is a lie. Not by deliberate misinformation but by omission. It omits mention of the significant contributions that people of color have made to this nation. It attempts to render us invisible but finds that it can't. Yet even in the face of this failure it continues to try, and try and try again.

Chorus:

Giovanni's Room . . . The Devil Finds Work . . . A Rap on Race, with Margaret Mead . . . A Dialogue with Nikki Giovanni . . . Nothing Personal, photography by Richard Avedon . . . If Beal Street Could Talk . . . Another Country . . . One Day When I Was Lost . . . Nobody Knows My Name . . . Going to Meet the Man . . . No Name on the Street . . .

All these books were written to give voice to a people who refused to be silenced.

Baldwin:

Mine is one voice among many, and I try to raise it loud and clear as I did many years ago as a boy in my father's church. I started out with gospel then moved on to the blues. But as you can see I never really left gospel, it is too much a part of me. So I'm singing it now before you, hoping that you'll all join in. A writer has only one voice, but that's a start. A preacher has one voice too. When the writer becomes a preacher or the preacher becomes a writer, you have the hybrid that stands before you now.

I was asked to come here and speak of my life and I think I have.

My life thus far has been one long wait. Waiting for the dream of America's deliverance to become a reality. I'm still waiting.

Chorus:

He started out in Harlem and ended up in France. Wrote *Notes of a Native Son,* an American native son—James Baldwin.

JOE LOUIS
(1914–1981)

Regarded by many as the finest heavyweight champion in the history of boxing, Mr. Louis held the world heavyweight title from 1937 to 1948, producing a division record of twenty-five successful title defenses—longer than anyone else in the history of the sport. He is best remembered for his rematch with Max Schmeling, a fighter who had previously defeated him. This time the fight took on all sort of political resonances: via Adolph Hitler, Schmeling became the representative of Aryan superiority and Louis the symbol of American toughness. It was a heavy responsibility to bear, but Louis shouldered it and was victorious in the bout. His photo was used on World War II recruiting posters. While in the army he fought many exhibition bouts and donated his purses to the war effort. Always patriotic and quietly decent and self-effacing, Louis never blamed his country's government for the tax problems he was saddled with for many years. He is still viewed today as one of the great American heroes who inspired the nation at a time when it needed a hero.

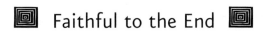 Faithful to the End

Joe Louis, age fifty-nine, his body softened and his speech and movement slowed, enters, hesitantly looks over the audience for a moment, and then begins to speak.

Joe:

Good evening [*afternoon*] everybody. They asked me to come here and tell you my story, and when I asked them why, they said "For the young people in our audience to learn from it."

"Learn what?" I asked myself. But I didn't say nothing to them.

The people who asked me here is smart people with all kinds of degrees, so they must know something I don't know. But it's been my experience that when you get past a certain age, it don't matter how famous you were or what you achieved, young people don't wanna hear nothing about it or you. They figure your time is passed and there ain't nothing you can say that will mean anything much to them. And I got to say, most of the times they right. The world and the things I wanna talk about is gone. And long gone too. Everything is changed. The buildings, the clothes people wear, the way young people talk and think. And even the style of boxing is changed from when I used to do it.

They tell me that I'm still a role model. In my day they called me a credit to my race. And then somebody added the human race. Well I have to tell you, in my day they called me all kinds of things: the Brown Bomber, the Detroit Assassin, and in some areas the Womb Wrecker. But I won't go into that here.

I guess what I have to say to young people, if they want to hear it, is, follow your dream, and don't let nobody tell you that you can't. America is a wonderful country even with all of its faults. If it wasn't, I wouldn't be standing here talking to you. I wouldn't a done what I done, been where I been, meet who I meet, and gotten what I have if it wasn't for this country. People say I'm too patriotic, and because of my patriotism it make me some kinda fool. I not only heard it from folks on the street but seen it written that way in papers and magazines. But far as I'm concerned, that's just their opinion, mine is completely different.

I growed up in a house of sixteen children, when most of the time there wasn't enough food to feed everybody. So every day, somebody had to do with less, and a lotta the times with no food at all. And that somebody always was my mother, Lillie Barrrow, who everybody, even her husband, my stepfather, called Miss Lillie. She was a woman of strength who had faith in the future.

(*Quoting his mother*) "It don't matter how bad things seem to be or what you hear them sayin' about us down South. There ain't nothing you can't do if you put your mind to it, son. As long as you alive and willing, you can do it, and don't let nobody discourage you, ever. We live in a world where for reasons I could never understand, people always want to break you down but never build you up. Always want you to know your place, and that place is always below them, you follow what I'm sayin'?"

"Yes, Mama."

"That's a boy, that's my big boy."

Her dream for me was to be a musician. She wanted me to play the violin. I know it sounds funny now, but that's what she hoped. And to make that dream come true, she took extra work washing and ironing other people's clothes to pay for the lessons. I went a few times, and then began to stray. There was a place across town where some friends used to go to exercise and learn to throw their hands. I started going with them and got to liking it. Got to liking it a lot. But I didn't tell Mama nothing about that, I didn't wanna break her heart or hurt her feelings. So when she asked how the lessons was coming, I always just said, "fine, Mama, just fine."

Then one day my lie got found out. The music teacher went to our house looking for me, asking why I hadn't been to my lessons. Mama was disappointed, I could see it on her face when she asked me about it. But she didn't complain or scold. All she said to me was, "Is this boxing thing what you want to do, Joe?"

"Yes, Mama."

"Then that's what you better do, Son. But how you gonna do it?"

"The best it can be done. Which means better that everybody else."

"That's my boy."

Pause.

My whole name was Joe Louis Barrow, but when I went to fill out the form for my fourth amateur bout there wasn't enough room on the line, so I just wrote Joe Louis and that became my name ever since.

In my first amateur fight I was knocked down seven times. None of my family was there too see it, thank god. But in my mind, I could hear Mama asking, "Is that the best you can do, Joe?" And I knew that it meant that I had to work harder and learn a lot more.

People like to say that boxers are dumb; I'd like to see them try it sometime. I don't mean just fooling around in the gym with your friends, but in the gym every day with trainers and people who are trying to make a living at it. Getting up early every morning to do roadwork, going to a regular job all day, then in the evening going to the gym to spar and hit the bag hours into the night before going home. And when you get home, being so tired that you hardly want to eat. All you want to do is sleep, so you can get up early and do the whole thing over again the next day. That's what the profession of boxing demands.

My first pro fight was in 1934 and I made fifty bucks. After eight more fights I got the nickname the Brown Bomber. One year after that fifty-dollar fight I was making sixty thousand dollars for fighting the heavyweight Primo Carnera. After I knocked him out, my boxing career took off like a rocket and the money just start pouring in. People say I was stupid with my money. I bought my mama a house. Tell me what was stupid about that. Put my brothers and friends in business. Help out people I knew to be in need. Started a softball team, bought them all uniforms and a bus to travel in. Bought myself a farm with horses, because I always loved horses and dreamed of owning and training them one day. But the thing that satisfied me the most was when I gave the city of Detroit a check for two hundred and fifty dollars as payback for the welfare checks they gave our family after my stepfather was hurt in a car accident. The way I see it is, that's why you work and try to make money, so you can help your family and friends. So when I made it, that's what I did. I did one other thing too at that time. I got married. So as far as I was concerned I had everything in life I wanted except one thing, the heavyweight championship of the world. I was beating everybody, knocking everybody out, but I needed the title. Everybody said so, even my trainer, Chappy.

"Boy, you can beat all the heavyweights they put in front of you from here to kingdom come. But if you don't beat the champ, and if you ain't the champ, none of the rest of it count for much."

To fight the champ I had to beat Max Schmeling, a German fighter people were saying had fast hands. I trained for Max and trained hard, too. People like to say that I didn't but I did. They like to say that I was taking it easy, living the good life too much, hanging out in nightclubs with too many musicians like Cab Calloway and Duke Ellington instead of training like I should. They said that fame and success had gone to my head. But that wasn't true.

Now before the fight nobody was saying any of that. In fact every-body was so sure that I was going to win that half the crowd they expected stayed home, figuring it would be a short fight. That I would knock him out in two or three rounds. Instead, what happened was he knocked me out in the twelfth round. Out for the count. And that's when the talk of me taking it easy started up. What nobody wanted to admit is that Max had my number that night. He was a step or two ahead of me all the time. A jab or two in front, and I couldn't catch him. And when the time came, he did what you're supposed to do in a fight like that. He came in for the KO and he got it.

Pause.

How did I feel after the fight? I felt like hell. I had let a lot of people down. First myself and then the black people of America. They was counting on me and I let them down. I didn't feel I could face them, because so many had bet their week's pay on me. And so many have used my victories to lift up their spirits when things were going bad for us coloreds in this country. I'll tell you I felt so bad that I went into hiding. I didn't even want to see my wife. It was Chappy Blackburn, my trainer, who finally sat me down and talked some sense into me.

"Joe, you lost a fight. One fight. An important fight it's true. But it still is only one fight. You got other fights in the future to think about and work for. You is only human. Other people lose and now it was your turn. And you can't worry too much about it. And you can't continue to hide yourself like you're doing. You gotta come out and face the world. Them people saying you let them down, they're looking for a hero. If it wasn't you it would be somebody else. You can't fill your head up with stuff like that. You gotta concentrate on the future and what you learned from this loss. Prize is still the heavyweight championship, and that's what we have to go after. So that's what we have to focus on from now on."

And that's what we did. Train hard and focus and when the time came one year later, against James Braddock, who was the champ, I was ready. Braddock fought hard, but I took him out in the eighth and I was *the heavyweight champion of the world*. I was twenty-three and the youngest heavyweight champion ever. And the first black heavyweight champion since Jack Johnson in 1908. But I wasn't satisfied. I had to fight Schmeling again. I had to know if he was better than me or if that KO was just a fluke. I even went so far as to tell people, "You can't call me champ until I beat Schmeling."

We signed for a rematch to happen on June twenty-second, 1938, at Yankee Stadium, where we had fought the first time. It was to be a fight between two men to prove who was the best at what they did. That's what it was supposed to be. But then the politicians got involved, and the next thing you know he was fighting for Germany and I was fighting for America. He was fighting to prove some point about Aryan superiority that Hitler was trying to make. Didn't either of us believe it was more than a prize fight, but everybody else built it into this big thing. Even President Franklin D. said in public, "Joe, we need muscles like yours to beat Germany." Once again the whole damn country was relying on me.

When the first bell rang I was prepared. I had studied his style and improved on my own. We're a little over a minute into the first round when I had him down. He got up but I put him down again two more times. With the third knockdown he was out. The fight was over, and for the first time in my mind I was the real heavyweight champion.

Pause.

I held on to the belt for over ten years, defended it twenty-five consecutive times, with twenty of those fights ending in KOs. No other champion has ever held on to it or defended it for that long. There were ups and downs. Divorces and bankruptcies. And a big mighty problem with the income tax people. But I still don't believe that what I accomplished could have been done in any other country but this. And that's why I love it. And that's why I'll always be faithful to it.

So what should you young people take away from this talk? That a person should always be faithful to something. In my case it was the country in which I was born. Thank you for listening.

He exits.

JOSEPH CINQUE (?)

Joseph Cinque was a twenty-five-year-old rice farmer from Sierra Leone, West Africa, who was captured and bound into slavery in 1839. Cinque (African name, Singbe-pieh) and many other Africans were taken to Cuba, where they were sold to a Spaniard named José Ruíz. They were placed on a schooner called the *Amistad* (*Friendship*) so they could be 'transported to another part of the island. That night, during a storm at sea, the slaves broke free and, under the leadership of Cinque, took over the ship. They eventually landed in the United States, where the abolitionist movement took up their cause for freedom. It became a celebrated event and pitted ex-president John Quincy Adams against the sitting president, Martin Van Buren.

Cinque was a fascinating and contradictory man whose appearance, intelligence, and personality made him a star attraction everywhere he went. The fight for his freedom and that of the other slaves was conducted in three trials, the final one in the Supreme Court, in Washington, D.C., where John Quincy Adams passionately argued for the right of the slaves to be free. He won the case, and they were ultimately returned to their homes in Africa.

The story of fifty-three slaves whose demand for freedom was heard by the Supreme Court is significant because it forced the United States to confront the true meaning and responsibility of its own Declaration of Independence. It was the first battle cry for freedom that ultimately led to the Civil War.

 Memories of the *Amistad*

The year is 1839. Joseph Cinque, age twenty-five, is dictating his recollections to an unseen scribe. His English is uncertain and heavily accented.

Cinque:

You ask what I remember. I remember the sea and weather. Boat tossin' and turnin'. Tossin' and turnin' over, but not turnin' over. Then turn to other side. And then turn and turn again. Bad weather. Bad weather and bad men. Bad men who chain us and beat us. Bad men who take us from homeland and kill some of us. Bad men who laugh and make us dance. Bad men who call us names we don't understand.

Bad weather go on. Wind blowin' hard. We hear bad men upstairs shoutin' and cryin'. We in dark hole below gettin' sick. Everybody, everybody sick. Me too. Everybody make big mess. Hole smell bad. Very bad. Everybody afraid boat sink, everybody drown. Can't move. Chains too tight. We pull, pull hard, chains too strong, cut skin. Everybody cryin' and crazy. Boat still turnin' and turnin'. Wind still blowin' and blowin'. Things falling everywhere. Fire and water comin' in. Too much things fallin'. Can't hide. Everybody duck. Things still hit. Boat still goin' up and down and not want to stop.

Don't know what to do. Hate this boat. Hate men of the boat. Men who take us from homeland with ropes and whips. Men who push us and kick us. Give us food but spit in it. Bad men with white skin and long hair who keep us in dark all day. Who sometimes take one of us upstairs and we never see him again.

Pause.

Boat still tossing. Nobody know what to do. Everything in hole rollin' and wet. All of us sicker. All of us still pullin' the chain. I get a nail. Nail from wood that break off boat. I look at it, nail is long and sharp. I play with nail, nail is hard. Lock is not far. I put nail in lock like key. Lock they use to hold chain. Lock they put on when they go upstairs. Boat still turnin' but I still keep nail in lock. Boat now turnin' slow and slower. Wind stop blowin'. No more noise upstairs. Everybody must be tired. In hole everybody still sick. All close eyes to sleep.

Pause.

I wake up, everybody still asleep. Boat very quiet now. Boat not even movin' and nobody come down to look at us. I still have nail in lock, movin' it movin' it. Hear a noise. Click. Lock open. I look around, everybody still asleep. Don't know any of these men, all from different tribes. All speak language I don't understand. But all chain together, all eat together, all throw up together, all suffer together, all black like me.

I move the lock and pull chain free. Wake up man next to me. Pull his chain free. His name Grabeau. We talk a little. He wake man next to him. Pull his chain free. We wake up everyone, tell them to be quiet and pull all chain free. No noise upstairs, no noise downstairs either. Hour is late at night. I creep upstairs to peep. Look on deck. Everybody sleeping. Moon is bright. And boat just rockin' side to side. Deck have things all over it. I see sword and take it. See other sword, take that too. Then I see knife and wood. Take them and still nobody wake. I go back down. Everybody quiet and waiting. I give them sword, knife, and wood. We go back upstairs quiet and chop bad man sleeping. Then chop another and another. Still no noise, still nobody wake. Then we chop other and other and other. Everybody on deck choppin' now and noise begin. Lot a noise. Fightin' and blood now. Shoutin' and cursin'. Blood, blood everywhere. Fightin' everywhere. Everything is confusion, but we keep fightin'. Bad men fight back. Some run to hide. We are many and all over the boat. Sword in hands, fightin' and choppin'. Boat captain, Captain Ferrer, fight good, fight hard, kill many of us. Four men catch him. Chop chop chop him. Chop him up good.

When captain die others give up. Some we chop, some we put overboard in boat. Blood everywhere on deck. People slippin' and fallin' down on blood but nobody care. Boat is ours. Everybody eatin' and drinkin' now. Everybody laughin' and throwin' things in the air.

I look at everything; we need order. But nobody care. Everybody drunk and laughin'. I look at the sun, it bright and burnin'. Boat is just goin' with nobody in control. We need somebody to sail boat. But everybody drunk, nobody care.

I go to captain's room, look at everything. See maps but can't read them. See books and glass and gold and rum and clothes. Captain clothes. I look at them in mirror. Put jacket on. Look at mirror again. I am captain. Man with captain's clothes is captain. I am he.

I go back on deck and men have Mr. Ruíz and Mr. Montes in chains. They find them hiding on deck. Men goin' to chop them up. I stop it, show them captain jacket, I am captain. All agree. Three who don't agree, I point, say, "Throw them overboard," and others obey. They throw them overboard. Now everybody know I am captain.

Mr. Montes and Mr. Ruíz very frighten of chop chop. Montes already hurt, head bleedin'. I tell Ruíz I save their live if he read map and sail us to homeland. He say yes. I tell him to teach people how to make sail go up and down and how to sail boat too. He shake head yes. I tell him if any trick, we chop him up. He know we mean it. He see us do it. Then I tell everybody we goin' home. Everybody happy. I am good captain.

Pause.

Days and days pass. Something not right. Ruíz tryin' tricks. Boat is sailing away from sun. Sun is where homeland is. Other agree with me. When we sail here it was away from sun. To sail home we must sail into sun. I take sword and tell Ruíz to turn boat around. He do it.

I am captain but I have assistants. I appoint them. Grabeau is number two. He older, very sensible. He talk with Montes and Ruíz, understand what they say, and tell me. He talk to me, understand what I say, and talk to them. Grabeau very smart. I glad he here. Two, three others good, but not smart like Grabeau.

Everybody drink too much. Some fight. Women and babies cry all the time. More fights. I stop the fightin' and say anyone who fight more go over in water. All fighting stop. Montes and Ruíz talk too much to each other. I put one upstairs and one downstairs. No more talk. I don't trust them.

At night I look at moon and dream of homeland. Grabeau say he dream of homeland too. Dream of wife and children before bad men come and take him away. I dream of woman too. Not wife, woman. No children. But when I get back, maybe. I dream of land, house, and homeland food. I dream of my life before bad man come and take me away. Dream of everything I ever want to see again. But we be home soon. Very soon.

Pause.

Trouble and more trouble. Stupid people eat all food. Now no more food. People want captain to make more food. People drink all water. People want captain to make water fall from sky. People stupid. People want captain to be god. Captain not god. But I tell them we get home soon, plenty of food and water there. People say they want water now, want food now. Children cry all the time, women moan, and men get drunk. Captain don't know what to do.

Grabeau point to island, say we get food and water there. Ship is dirty, very dirty. I tell them to clean ship. They say they want food. I tell them clean deck, I get food. Everybody have knife, everybody have sword, everybody dangerous. Montes and Ruíz frighten. Think they get chop chop. I tell them no. Tell them I am captain. Ask how close to homeland we be. Soon, they tell me, very soon. I tell them I keep order. Everybody obey me even stupid people.

Pause.

We go to island. Island people even more stupid than boat people. Throw rocks and spears at us. We try to show them black skin. Black skin like theirs. Island brothers, homeland brothers, one an' same. All one people, black. Stupid people not listen. Throw spears and fire at us. We run. But get water and food. Not much, little. But it something.

Back in ship again. Sailing, sailing, sailing, but no homeland. Ruíz say soon, soon. Ruíz is liar I think but not sure. Grabeau say is smart, tricky. Say we should watch close. Montes say nothing now, sick all the time. Boat stink. Nobody clean even though captain tell them. Food runnin' out again. See other boat. We wave, they sail away quick. Nobody stop. Bad weather again. Rain, wind, high seas. Everybody hide. Everybody afraid. Grabeau, captain, and Ruíz keep ship up. Big sail fall down kill man. Other sail fall down, kill other man. Weather bad night and day, night and day. Then wind stop, sea quiet again. Everybody angry, say captain is bad luck. That captain should die. Need new captain. But everybody too sick, everybody too weak. So captain stay in charge. Captain tell Ruíz that no homeland in two days, captain will chop chop.

Pause.

Captain don't feel so good. Captain have fever. Grabeau help, he sail boat with Ruíz while captain sleep. He watch Ruíz for tricks.

People on boat not so stupid. People help each other and help captain too. But too many weak and sick. Boat need food and water. Some jump in sea and die. Maybe we all die before seein' homeland. Maybe our ancestors take us back home through the air. Or under the sea. Or maybe back in dreams and smoke. Better to die and go with ancestors than live and work in chains for bad men.

New day, Grabeau wake me. "Land," he say, "land." On deck we see land. See other boats too. Many other boats. We show Ruíz and Montes. Ruíz say good place for water and food. Captain and Grabeau with others take small boat with gold for food.

On land everybody look at us. Look at captain jacket. We show them gold, point to food and water. They take gold, give us food. Plenty food, plenty water too. Feel better now. People white but not so bad. Fill boat with water and food. Go back to big boat.

We go on boat, soldiers meet us. Ruíz and Montes point and soldiers come for me. I look, everybody in chains. "No more chains," I think and jump overboard. I swim and dive, swim and dive, but too much boats around. Captain jacket too wet, too heavy, can't swim anymore. Man pull captain from sea. "Welcome to America," he say, "you under arrest."

Pause.

Place is call America. Place is call New London. Captain and everybody is call fugitive slaves . . . savage, wild Africans . . . black ghost. I say my name is Singbe-pieh. They call me Cinque. Call my ship *Amistad*. Walk us through street, everybody look at us. Put us in jail. Women and children too. Many still weak and sick. Not strong like captain.

Captain wrong. White people not good. White people bad.

Captain in jail with food and water. Montes and Ruíz look at us, laugh, and talk with soldiers. "U.S. Navy," soldiers say.

Many days pass. Different white people come see us. Tell us they abolitionists.

"Who is abolitionists?"

Say they is group who want to free slaves. Who want to send Singbe and others back to homeland. Say Mr. Montes want to take us back to Cuba, as his property. Say Montes and Ruíz tell how we kill captain and everybody. Say we bad, but we belong to him. Abolitionists say no man belong to other. Judge in court say we stay in jail until law decide.

I see now. Abolitionists is good white people. They come to jail every day, bring food for us, and medicine people who help the sick. Try to talk to Grabeau and me. But we don't understand, they don't understand. Newspaper talk about us. But time pass and pass. Everybody in jail, but everybody comfortable. Children play outside, women smile and show good white people our dances and chants.

Missionary people tell us about god. Different god from African god. Say this is the true god. God that will deliver us back to homeland if we believe. We want to get back to homeland, so we say we believe. Missionary very happy.

People like to see Singbe stand and show self. So Singbe show self. People give him clothes and paint his picture. People give Singbe special food, special treatment. People say Singbe special. Singbe look at mirror, Singbe is special. People study me, say Singbe is too special to be slave. Too intelligent, too strong.

They find man who can talk to us. Black sailor named Covey, he tell us what they say and tell them what we say. Talkin' better now. Don't take so much time. He say our case very important. Everybody talkin' about it. Say a group call friends of the *Amistad*. Workin' hard for us. People line up to see us every day. And the boss of our jail is chargin' money for the people to look at us. People pay.

They put me in a special jail and take me out to show me to people. Fancy white man come say he takin' *Amistad* case to high district court. Tell us, "America is for freedom. Freedom for everyone, including you. We're gonna win this case," he say, "because God is on our side."

So this is now. We go to high court tomorrow.

Pause.

America is funny country. It put you in jail but treat you good. Tie you with chain, but tell you everybody is free. We ask to go to homeland, they say they take us to homeland. Then everybody talk and talk and talk. One court, two court, now this court. Everything confused. Good man, bad man, Montes, Ruíz, Tappan, Baldwin, sheriff, abolitionists, soldier, navy, black man, white man, free man, slave man. Everything confused.

We all tired. Grabeau, Singbe, everybody tired. We just want to go to homeland. Maybe tomorrow, after court. Maybe. We see.

DANIEL LOUIS "SATCH" ARMSTRONG (1900–1971)

Louis Armstrong, affectionately called Satch throughout most of his long career, was one of the most influential and famous of all jazz artists. It is said that his style of playing and singing has influenced every aspect of American music we hear.

He was born in the black ghetto of New Orleans. At thirteen he was sent to a reform school for a year. It was there that he learned to play cornet and read music. When he was released in 1915, Louis showed enough promise that King Oliver, a well-known band leader in the area, gave him lessons on the trumpet. In 1917, Armstrong moved to Chicago, and it was there that his professional career properly began. Two years later he moved to New York City and began his unique vocalizing along with playing the trumpet. Between 1925 and 1930, with various groups, Armstrong displayed a dazzling array of rhythmic inventions and improvisations that has yet to be matched. He changed styles and bands often, but his virtuoso playing of the trumpet and his unique style of singing, along with his bubbling, upbeat personality, kept audiences entranced. He became one of the best known and one of the most popular personalities all over the world. He was called America's Goodwill Ambassador wherever he went and through the years appeared in over thirty motion pictures, mostly playing himself.

Since his death in 1971, his reputation as a musician has grown to a point where he is frequently referred to as the Rembrandt of American music.

I met Louis Armstrong in 1969, two years before he died. I was thirty years old. The meeting came about this way. I was working in a flower shop as a delivery person. One day, his wife, Lucille, brought in a plant that was dying and asked if anything could be done to restore it. The guys who ran the place said yes and took it in. They clipped it, repotted it, fertilized it, and attended to it for close to three months. Then, on a day in

May, they called the Armstrong residence, asked if I could deliver the plant, and were told yes, that a check would be waiting.

I took a cab to the address and rang the bell. Mr. Armstrong himself answered, invited me in, looked at the plant, and was pleased. He said that his wife had become attached to the plant and she would be happy for its restoration when she returned. I said, "I'm glad you're pleased, Mr. Armstrong." And that's when he said, "Call me Louis, everybody does. Louis or Satch." We talked some more, and he asked if I was in the flower business. I told him that I wasn't, that I just worked in delivery, but I was studying theatre at night in hopes of an acting career somewhere in theatre or film. He laughed and offered me a Coke, which I accepted. He sat down, and we talked for perhaps fifteen or twenty minutes. He was wearing a worn-out-looking robe and looked to be a little worn-out himself, but the voice was still distinctive and the smile was still there. What I've tried to do in this monologue is reproduce what he said as well as I remember it.

Riffing

Louis Armstrong, age sixty-nine, wearing a worn-out-looking robe, is sitting in a comfortable chair; as he talks he sips a soft drink.

Louis:

Acting. Son, that's an art that I respect but could never master. Still, though, they let me get into a whole lot of movies playing myself. In the beginning, I used to try to act and try to pretend that I was somebody else, but it just wouldn't work. For one thing, I was always forgetting my lines. I can remember all the words of more than a dozen songs in any concert, but give me more than two or three lines to say together and the whole thing would go out of my mind no matter how hard I worked on it. And it would hold up everybody while I messed up take after take after take. In the end, the director would just tell me, "Say it your way, Louis." And when

I did, they could move on. So I had to put in my contract that I wouldn't be learning anything long to say in any movie I was in. Everybody agreed and let me make one picture after another.

Now the one time I did try to do a little acting was in the movie *Paris Blues*, where I was supposed to be playing another trumpet player, not Louis Armstrong. I worked a lot of days and hours on it, and the director, Mr. Ritt, he worked with me too. When it was time to shoot, I did most of it without holding up anybody. A year later when the picture came out, the critics said I did a nice job. I was real pleased. Then a few years later, I was in some city, and it was playing around the corner from my hotel. So I went to see it. What I saw on the screen wasn't acting. It was me playing myself, only with a different name. Maybe that's what acting is all about. I don't really know.

Pause.

I think my favorite movie to make was *High Society*. I always have fun whenever I get together with Bing Crosby. Frank Sinatra too. In that picture, I even got to play and sing some music from your part of the world, Cole Porter style. They called it the High Society Calypso. Let me see, I had a good time with Danny Kaye in *The Five Pennies*. His wife wrote some nice stuff for us in that picture.

Pause.

Ella [*Fitzgerald*] is my dream girl. Always been. Sing like an angel and quick on her feet musically. Anything you throw at her, she's ready for. She'll take it, do something different with it, then throw it back at you. Sometimes just to be evil, I'd throw stuff at her just to see if I could catch her off guard. I ain't ever succeeded so far. She is the best of the best.

Pause.

I like the way young people operate these days. They try a lot of things, then later on settle down on one. When I was young, I wasn't that way. Music was the only thing to occupy me. Played it in the morning, lunchtime, in the evening, and sometimes all through the night 'til the crack of day.

Pause.

Playing the horn is tiring, especially now at my age. So before I go out for a concert, I try to take a long nap, just so's I can have the energy for a full session. Then after we're done, if I don't have some-place important to go, I turn in early and try to get a full night's sleep. When I was young, I could play and stay up all night. Not anymore. Bones ache, and my back just won't take it no more.

Pause.

My music is jazz, but I play and sing every kind of music so long as I've got a pretty melody and some nice words to go with it. My mother used to say, "God smiles down on them that make the world smile." And that's what I try to do with my music and how I act when I'm up on stage. I try to make the world smile.

Pause.

It's been a nice career and I can't complain. I met up with all kinds of wonderful people. Presidents, kings, washerwomen, cabdrivers, car-penters, ditchdiggers, and everybody you can think of. People you would've never guessed that a poor boy from New Orleans would ever get to meet. But you know who I love the most? The children. The children and the musicians I played with. Wherever I go in the world, Europe, India, Africa, the faces of the children I meet and the questions they ask always make me happy. And I believe that all musicians are special. See, you gotta remember that the archangel Gabriel is a musician too. You ever stop and wonder why?

He laughs and exits.

MAHALIA JACKSON
(1911–1972)

Born in New Orleans, Louisiana, and raised on the banks of the Mississippi Delta, Mahalia Jackson was perhaps the greatest gospel singer America has ever known. Almost single-handedly she brought black gospel music from the churches of Chicago to the capital cities of the world. She sang at Carnegie Hall and the White House and sold millions and millions of records. All during her forty-five-year career Mahalia fought and campaigned for the rights of African Americans through her activities and through her music.

I wrote two monologues for Mahalia Jackson, then couldn't decide which one to include. So I kept them both; they capture Mahalia at different times in her life.

The Honest-to-God Truth
(young Mahalia)

Mahalia Jackson (called Hallie), age thirty-six.

Hallie:

Know what just happened? They just told me on the phone that my recording of "Move On Up a Little Higher" just passed a million copies in sales. I should be jumping for joy, right? But the truth is I ain't.

Oh, it ain't that I'm not happy about the record sales and all. Or about the fact that my concerts are selling out, or that every time I go to some church to praise the Lord, like I been doing every day of my life, the church benches fill up, people fill the back, and some even sit in the windows, just because I am there. "One of these days you are going to be the most popular woman in the world," Harry, that white fellow that want to handle my contracts, said to me. "You're almost there now."

The other day a fellow did a newspaper article on me that was called "She's Got the Whole World at Her Feet." Everybody I know thinks that's the story of my life. And I don't tell them any different, 'cause that's what they want to believe. They want to believe that money and fame is the key to joy and happiness. And I can't say I blame them, because I used to believe it too. When I was a girl and I heard Bessie Smith on the radio singing them songs, I used to think to myself, "Oh Lord, if I could only be like her, do what she's doing, and have people pay and cherish me just for singing. That would be heaven, and I wouldn't want anything more."

In those day I was only dreaming and didn't believe that nothing like that could ever happen to me. I was just this poor child lonely and lost most a the time. My mama was dead and my father was away with another wife who didn't want to know nothing about me. So I had to live with my Aunt Duke. She was a woman who lived for only two things, God and hard work. And when I sing at the church she said to me, "Child, God give you a voice that come straight from the angels. And that voice is for you to worship and praise Him every day of your life." So what that mean is that I couldn't sing blues or any other kind of popular music. Only hymns.

It was my cousin Chafalaya, that everybody said was no good, who was the one who said to me, "Girl, you wastin' your time at this backwater place. What you gotta do is come to Chicago with me. With your voice and my smarts we could make us a pot of money." That was the first time I ever thought that maybe I could make a living by singing. But Fala was too fast and too flashy for me. So I told him no and he went off without me. He wasn't gone long when we got the news that he was dead. Somebody shot him in the heart during a dice game.

Pause.

While everybody was moaning and praying at his wake I was remembering one of the other things he said to me, "Hallie, you gotta believe me. Chicago ain't nothin' like you ever seen. Tall buildings everywhere, wide streets, and black folks walkin' around like they own the place. If that ain't paradise, baby, it sure as hell is close to it."

Soon as I was sixteen I put on my Sunday hat, pack a box with my little bit of clothes, kiss Aunt Duke goodbye, and was on my way to the Windy City. My dream was to be a nurse, help sick people get better, then find a man to marry and have a whole houseful of children. But it turn out that Fala was right. My destiny was in my singing. I did a little bit of it in the church, and the next thing I knew people was asking me to join their group, offering me money to tour with them. The Johnson Singers was a group I hooked up with and stayed with the longest. Then when they broke up, I went out on my own. The money started coming in so I was able to help poor Aunt Duke and my other family people back home. But every time I saw her the first thing she would ask is, "Hallie, is you praising your Lord?"

"Yes, Auntie."

"And you not following bad company is you?"

"No, Auntie."

"Good. That's my baby. That's my little girl."

Pause.

One day on the street a man just walked up and talked to me. When I wouldn't answer back he said I must be from the country, because here in the city people know that it's civilized to answer when somebody talk to you. I told him I was civilized but that I didn't talk to strange men on the street. So he introduced himself. Told me his name was Isaac Huckenhull but that most folks called him Ike. We walk and talk and the next thing I know he was showing me the sights of the city. Sights I had never seen even though I was living there four years already.

We saw each other off and on for nearly a year. When I asked what he did for a living, he told me, "A little of this and a little of that." At the moment he was working for the post office, but the place he was spending most of his time was at the racetrack. In other words, Ike Huckenhull was a gambling man.

I wasn't surprised when he asked me to marry him. But I was

surprised that I said yes. I knowed that he wasn't perfect, but he was exciting and carried himself in such a way that it made me proud just to be with him. I remember what he said the first time he heard me sing. He said, "Halia, girl, you don't just talk about singin'. Honey child, you really do it." Then he told me that he loved me. That was the first time in my life that a man ever said those words to me. And didn't nobody have to ask if I loved him. I think every inch of my body showed it when he was near. So we got married. He was thirty I was twenty.

Things went smooth for a while. He was working and I was getting paid to sing. I was singing everywhere, all over this country. One day Louis Armstrong came right to our home and asked me to sing with his band. But I had to tell him no, because that would mean singing something other than gospel. When Ike heard it he was mad as hell, "Girl, ain't you got no sense? Gospel is a dead end. A street with nowhere to go, blues and jazz is where it's at right now. So that's what you should be doing. You've gone about as far as anybody has gone in gospel, but still we ain't got no real money comin' in."

"We ain't got no money," I said to him, "because every dime or dollar we make you gamble away on one sport or another."

"Life is a gamble," he said to me, "and if you don't know that, you still have a whole lot to learn."

Time went on and I began to make even more money than he could spend. I was away a lot and he was staying home. There was rumors about Ike and other women. Lots of other women. But there is always rumors of one kind or another about men like Ike, so I didn't pay too much mind. Because when we were together Ike always gave me his undivided attention.

But this gambling thing was bothering me more and more. It wasn't just the money. Lord knows I was making enough. It was the whole business of gambling itself. Ever since I was small I was brought up to think of it as evil. The devil's work. And every woman I knew in Louisiana or Chicago who was breaking her back doing some kind of lowdown job to keep food on the table so her children could eat, was because she was married or involved with some kind of gambling no-account lowlife. Add to that the fact that my favorite cousin, Fala, was killed during a dice game made me hate gambling even more. So I couldn't ignore it when I saw how addicted

Ike was to it. I didn't want him to end up like Fala, and I didn't want to be one of those women always complaining about their husband's wandering ways. So one day I said to him, "Ike this gambling gotta stop. I'm working like an animal on all these long tours, singin' my guts out just so you can put it on a horse or the roll of a dice. I am a God-fearing woman and I just ain't gonna have it anymore. I would rather put the money I earn into the poor box than have you throw it away like that."

He look at me with a kinda sorry look on his face and for the first time I could see that he was getting on in age. I was thirty-five and he was forty-five, but his hair was almost all white already and the lines on his face was getting longer and deeper.

"You don't give a man much choice, do you," he said. "In fact you don't give him any choice at all."

"What do you mean by that?" I asked. "Answer me, what do you mean?"

But he didn't answer and the next thing I knew he was packed and out of the house. Gone and I was sitting there on the bed all by myself.

I didn't know what to do. I didn't mean for him to up and leave like that. But I also wasn't going to run out after him. I wasn't wrong. So I wasn't going to chase him when he is the one who should be apologizing to me and promising to change his ways. His problem is he was just too proud. Too damn proud.

Just when this was all going on I had to leave on a concert tour. This time it was in Europe. And everywhere I played, the crowds got bigger and bigger and more enthusiastic. I didn't know that Frenchmen and Swedish folks and Danish people and Englishmen could like gospel so. But I guess they all got spirits that can be moved, and somehow me and my music was doing just that.

Before I left I wrote down the schedule of every place I was going to be and left it in the house and with several people I knew, and every stop we made during that tour I would search my mail hoping to get a letter from Ike. But none ever came. When I got back home I heard that he had gotten a lawyer, so I got me one too. And that was that. He signed the divorce papers, I signed them too, and it was over. Nearly thirteen years of marriage down the drain. I didn't want it to be like that. It was as if things had just took on a life of their own and there was nothing I could do about it, I just had to ride it out.

Ike is gone but I still love him. Love him more now than ever. Or so it seem. And I can't tell you how lonely it is when I go to that empty house and that empty bedroom that we used to share.

Every night when I'm singing, people clap and blow me kisses. Everybody tells me how wonderful I am. And then I go home to that house and the loneliness sets in. It's funny, it seems like the more success I have the lonelier I get. It's like the good Lord made it so I would be loved by millions but somehow couldn't get the love of one man. I'm not complaining, because I'm not ungrateful, and I'm not even asking why. The Lord works in mysterious ways they say, and I guess this is what they mean. But you want to know something? I would give it all up if I could get what most of you have, or seem to have, without even trying. And that is the honest-to-God truth.

◫ Why I Sing Gospel ◫

A bare stage with one chair off to the side. Bessie Smith's recording of "I Hate to See That Evening Sun Go Down" is heard in the background. Mahalia, fifty-nine or sixty years old, is sitting, listening to it. She hums along and picks up on the vocal for a few bars, then begins to speak as the music fades out.

Mahalia:

People always asking me why I only sing gospel. Some even went so far as to try and tempt me with money and other stuff if I would sing jazz or blues. But I ain't ever slipped, and I ain't ever wavered. Gospel is my music and gospel is what I sing.

Now to me the greatest blues singer who ever lived was Bessie Smith. And as a child I used to listen to her records whenever I could and try to imagine what it must be like to open my mouth and make the kind of music that could reach the hearts and minds of so many people. I used to image it and dream it, but the blues wasn't for me. I wasn't born to that kind of rhythm. Our Baptist church didn't have no organ and no trumpets or no piano neither. Just a preacher saying words with the faithful clapping hands and humming and a true saved sister beating on a tambourine.

In the distant background we hear humming and a tambourine. Mahalia listens for a moment and begins to clap her hands in time.

That was the music that stirred my blood and fired my soul. That's the music that set my heart singing and it ain't stopped yet. And I ain't stopped neither. Gospel has been good to me and I ain't got no reason not to be faithful. People say to me all the time, "Oh, Halia, because of you America is singing gospel music in the morning and night, and they even singing it at Christmas time. And singing it, too, in times of trials and tribulations. You have made gospel music a part of our lives." They tell me that all the time. And I admit I had a hand it it. Oh yes, a big hand. But Halia ain't the only one. No sir, not at all. Right now there are more than eight hundred gospel singing groups touring and playing to packed churches and concerts all over this country. The Lord God Almighty has always been popular. I am just but one voice carrying his word.

Still others ask: "Why do you just sing gospel? Why don't you sing other music, too?" Well I've tried to answer that over and over. Let me see if I can by telling you a little story.

Some years ago I met a young man. He was a talker and a dreamer. And he could make the rocks move and the oceans swell with the sound of his voice and the power of his words. His name was Martin King. Martin Luther King. A young man from Georgia who loved his mama's cooking and some lively music when he was worshipping his Maker. We used to talk all the time, and he used to ask me to sing all the time. Then our paths got separated. His business took him in one direction, my business took me in another. I started out in Chicago, moved on to New York and Carnegie Hall, and then on to Paris, London, Germany, and all over the world. Then after I got sick, I had to come back home and settle down quiet for a while. That was the Lord telling me I was doing too much and pushing this tired body a little too hard. Oh, I wasn't ready to give up or nothing like that. No, I was just going to sit in my kitchen and let things take their own time as far as career and future was concerned.

And I was doing just that. Cooking and spending time with family and friends. Making a few recordings when the spirit moved me. Even went to Hollywood and made me a movie during this time. No, I didn't act no part. I was singing. Singing the word of the Lord up on that big silver screen. So like I was saying, everything was quiet and fine. Then one day I got a call. It was from Martin, who I hadn't seen in a number of years. He was calling to invite me to this march he was organizing—this march to the Lincoln Memorial, in Washington, D.C. Now I had been to Washington a couple of years before. John Kennedy had asked me to sing as his inauguration, and that was some honor for a little girl born by a river in New Orleans, Louisiana. But to be invited to this event by Mr. King was an even bigger honor.

"Halia," he said to me, "I got a special favor to ask. I want you to sing. I want you to sing like you never sung before. The date is August twenty-eighth. The place is Washington, D.C. I want you to go out there before I speak. I want you to calm them down for me. Think you could do that?"

"I'll certainly try," I told him. "I'll certainly try."

The morning was overcast and the advance word was that not many people would show up. They expected only a few hundred. Then around eleven the sun came out and the people began to pour in. Not by tens or hundreds, but by the thousands and thousands. Well over a quarter of a million was there. And it wasn't just black folks. White folks, green folks, red folks, and blue folks. All kinds of people. And the time came for me to sing. And for the first time in I don't know how many years, I was nervous. Really, really nervous. Everything was so quiet. Everybody was just standing there waiting. All those millions of people.

Pause. She stands looking at an empty spotlight center stage.

I opened my mouth and the words started to come.

We hear her recording of "I've Been 'Buked and I've Been Scorned."

Then all in a flash it was over. The place explodes like thunder. I didn't know where I was. Somebody led me off stage. Then Martin went out and spoke.

Pause. In the background we hear the end of MLK's "I Have a Dream" speech.

After that speech, if I didn't know before, I knew then why I had to sing gospel. And why I am going to go on singing it right to the end of my days.

We hear the sound of another Mahalia Jackson recording as she stands there listening and the lights begin to fade.

MALCOLM X
(1925–1965)

Malcolm X was born Malcolm Little in Omaha, Nebraska. His father, Earl, was a Baptist minister and a vocal supporter of the Black Nationalist leader Marcus Garvey. Because of this, he received death threats from the white supremacist group the Black Legion. To escape them, Earl moved his family to Lansing, Michigan. But two years later, his body was found lying dead across the town's railroad tracks.

Malcolm was a bright and alert student. He graduated from junior high school first in his class but lost interest in school when a favorite teacher told him that his ambition to become a lawyer was an unrealistic goal for a negro. Shortly after that he dropped out of school and drifted into crime. In 1946 he was arrested, convicted, and sentenced to ten years in prison for burglary. While in prison, he began to study the teachings of Elijah Muhammad and quickly converted to the Nation of Islam religion. By the time he was paroled in 1952, Malcolm was a devoted follower. He also changed his last name from Little to X in order to signify his lost identity.

After a few public appearances, Malcolm became the best-known speaker for the Nation of Islam. He was so charismatic that he is credited with increasing the organization's membership from five hundred in 1952 to thirty thousand in 1963. He became controversial because what he preached was the opposite of Martin Luther King's philosophy of nonviolence. He exhorted blacks to hate the white man for what he had done to them. He encouraged blacks to use violence to counter the violence perpetrated against them. In time, his popularity and fame eclipsed that of Elijah Muhammad. He was also subjected to much government surveillance, particularly by the FBI.

After a break with the Muslims, in which he was publicly critical of Elijah Muhammad's moral character, Malcolm went to Mecca, where the things he saw and people he encountered altered his view of racial relations. When he returned he was a profoundly changed man. "I met blond-haired, blue-eyed men I could call my brothers." He created a new organization that he said would work to build bridges between all races. But his days were numbered. He had received many death threats. And on February 21, 1965, at the Audubon Ballroom, where he was giving a public lecture, Malcolm was shot fifteen times. His three convicted assassins were all members of the Nation of Islam.

Today he stands alongside Martin Luther King as one of the greatest leaders of the civil rights movement.

 Changes

Malcolm X, age thirty-nine, is sitting at a small table, talking quietly to friends.

Malcolm:

As time passes, the world turns and changes. Seasons go one from another and then come back around again. Old buildings crumble and fall, while new ones rise. And the small seeds planted yesterday become large trees tomorrow. And so it is with a human heart and mind. It grows; it expands and becomes capable of embracing new ideas and concepts. And because of this ability we become wiser and healthier, thank Allah.

Pause.

I called you here this morning to deliver what's in my heart, before I announce it in a public forum. You are my loyal friends and followers and I have sought comfort in your warmth and friendship during my most trying times. You have never let me down. In my private moments of reflection and meditation I often ask myself how I've come to deserve such confidence and loyalty. I still don't have an answer, but I want you all to know that I am very, very grateful for it.

Pause.

America is a troubled land, a violent land. It was seized and settled by violence and continues to be ruled by the principles of violence. All of our coins and all of our currencies are printed with the statement, "In God we trust." But if the rulers in Washington and all the other so-called halls of justice were honest, what our currency would say is, "In violence we trust, and by violence we rule."

I became well-known and controversial because I said it was time, well past time, for our black brothers and sisters to stand up and strike back when struck. Because the white people who oppose us are either too hypocritical or too dumb to understand what is meant when we turn the other cheek. I said what I said because I was tired of seeing black people persecuted, hurt, and murdered. I wanted to see petrifaction and fear on the white man's face for a change.

I called him a devil because only a devil could do what he is doing to us for so many centuries and years. I said that the white man is a devil, and I will not retreat from that position. I will continue calling him a devil until the unequal treatment of us and the inhumane acts against us here in this country stop. And the white people who resent me for branding them with that label should turn their anger on those who commit these evil deeds in their name.

When I made statements like that, I was speaking of the majority. But in every general majority there are always exceptions. I have met many of these exceptions. White people who were courteous and gentle, generous and kind. People who were sensitive to the pain and suffering of others. I have met such people in my travels all over this country, and it has cheered me inside to know that such people exist. Still, for me, the world was America and America alone. And in light of all that was going on I saw no reason to point out the exceptions. They weren't in large enough numbers. But since I have been abroad I have seen many things that have affected me profoundly. Have walked, prayed, and exchanged ideas with people of many different races, cultures, backgrounds, and colors—and yes, including white. We have eaten together, laughed together, argued and helped each other together in more ways that I can recall or innumerate. Now, after such an experience, for me to remain as I was and continue speaking out publicly the way I had been would make me the most rigid, inflexible, and narrow-minded person in existence. Fortunately I flatter myself that I am not. And as you have heard me say over and over again, "I am nothing if not flexible. Flexible in all the proper meaning of the word."

That trip to Mecca expanded my outlook and altered the philosophy of what I believe. Because of what I saw and experienced, I can no longer subscribe to the idea of racism, be it white or black. It is too confining and self-defeating. There are good white people doing things to help mankind. To deny their humanity would be to deny my own. I have to acknowledge that they exist and I have to try to work with them.

This doesn't mean that I won't strike back at those who try to hurt or oppress me in any way. And I will encourage every black man and woman to do the same. But what I am abandoning is my old philosophy of violence and separation. I am now embracing a new position that includes listening to voices from many areas in our culture and our world. And to work toward building bridges of communication and support with our black brothers all over, especially Africa.

When I make this announcement, you're going hear a lot of flack from people who have always been critical of our movement. They're going tell you that I have been "bought out." That I have been co-opted and that I am intellectually unsure of what it is that I believe and subscribe to. This comes with the territory as you well know. Everything I have ever done or said has always been subjected to criticism and attack. That is the price of speaking out for what you believe, and I am not afraid to pay it.

With this change, of course, I see a new hope for the future of life for us all in this country and abroad. And because I do, I am very happy, despite all the negative forces that seem to be swirling around me everywhere I go. And because I am happy, I am very much at peace.

DR. MARTIN LUTHER KING JR.
(1929–1968)

Dr. King was the president of the Southern Christian Leadership throughout his career. He was born in Atlanta, Georgia, and held academic degrees from Morehouse College, Howard University, and Boston University. He was the author of several books and an architect of the nonviolent Civil Rights Movement. In 1964, he was awarded the Nobel Prize for Peace. In 1968, he was assassinated, in Memphis, Tennessee.

 ## I Want to Make This Clear

Martin, age thirty-six, is seated at a small table in shirt sleeves. It's 9:30 A.M. and he's tired from lack of sleep. He speaks softly, slowly, patiently.

Martin:

I called you here this morning to talk about something that has been disturbing me a lot. It has been bothering me for some time now. But for whatever reason, it came to a boil last night. I turned and turned but could only sleep in fits and starts. That's how troubled I was. Finally I became so restless that I got up so as not to waken my wife from her well-earned sleep. I went to another room, sat and looked at the walls for what seemed like hours on end.

The reason for this consternation is a repeated use of the phrase I am hearing all around me more and more by many members of our own organization as well as some of the other groups that we've partnered with. The phrase is *black power*. I don't like it, I never have. But to be fair in my assessment, I have tried to look at the term and what it means from several perspectives, because I could be wrong in my understanding and my outlook.

If I'm remembering correctly, the phrase was used in the writings of Richard Wright and a few others. And in that presentation it was meant to reverse the impression that anything black was ugly, undesirable, and hateful, while anything white was glorious, illuminating, and pristine. Wright and the others used the phrase to provide a sense of empowerment to people whose achievements have been belittled, stolen, or gone unheralded in this country. What they were saying is that our history is not just black history, it is American history. Our achievements and discoveries are not just black achievements and discoveries, they are larger than that. They encompass the entire spectrum of great achievements on the human scale.

It should be remembered that some of us dark-skinned African people were here on this continent long before Columbus arrived and long before a nation called the United States of America was formed. There were black sailors with Cortez in Mexico . . . black men with Balboa when he discovered the Pacific ocean . . . blacks when Coronado and his companions came upon the territory we now call New Mexico. It was Jean Baptiste, a black man, who founded the city of Chicago by building the first structure in that area.

Our list of achievements go on and on, and that is what the phrase *black power* was meant to convey in its original usage. That we are a powerful people who have contributed mightily to the growth of this nation and to the world at large.

But the recent usage of the phrase is one of anger and defiance. Its connotation is that of violence and destruction. When it is said, it is usually accompanied by a clenched fist brandished in the air. If that isn't a clear threat of violence, then I have no idea what a threat is.

Now I think I know where the feelings that make us want to talk like this come from. They come from anger and frustration at the slow progress we seem to be making in certain areas. From the resurgence of bigoted white power bases we see forming in the governments of so many states. From the brutal murders of our black and white civil rights marchers. And the overall feeling that everything we have gained has now somehow been taken back. One national magazine has even gone so far as to declare that our social revolution was nothing but a myth. And that our people today, despite all the laws enacted and the social programs introduced, are worse off than they were ten years ago. This of course is not true, but the illusion is there. And sometimes illusions are hard to dispel once they've taken hold.

Our movement is one of nonviolence. It always was and always will be as long as I have anything to do with it. From a religious and moral point of view, violence is wrong, it is ugly, and it is evil. To embrace and practice it would put us on the same level as our oppressors. It would demonstrate to the world that we are no better than they are and therefore not worth taking seriously. That we are just a bunch of wild savages and no more morally developed than the beasts of the jungle.

From the practical or pragmatic side of things embracing violence would also be counterproductive. It would provide those who hate us and the ones that support them the excuse they need to embark on a wholesale campaign of brutality and slaughter that would spread far beyond just the people in our movement. It would touch every black person in every walk of life in this country. They want a violent war and we are not equipped to fight such a war and win. We don't have the numbers, the weapons, or the expertise. So the notion, no matter how tempting or emotionally satisfying it might seem for the moment, is shortsighted and absurd. But more than that, it is morally reprehensible in the eyes of God and man.

We have come this far in our movement, and we have achieved what we have, because we have maintained a high moral ground in spite of everything they've tried to do to us. So this is no time to reverse ourselves. *Burn, baby, burn!* can only lead to destruction and despair. And taken to its furthest extreme I can imagine a battered landscape covered with smoking corpses and no living thing for miles and miles and miles. Because as I have said before and will probably say a thousand times more, the suggestion of "an eye for an eye" only leaves everyone blind.

We cannot condone violence, or give the impression that we do, with the use of phrases like *black power*. That is not our purpose and it will never be. Must never be. Because if it is, we will have lost all that we've gained in this long and painful struggle.

I said I wanted to make myself clear and I hope I have. This is where I stand, and I'm assuming that all here in this room are standing with me as well. And if you're not, the time to tell me is now.

He waits but gets no response.

Thank you. Now we can move forward with our plans and look to new horizons. God bless you all.

NAT TURNER
(1800–1831)

Preacher and rebel slave Nat Turner led the most successful and dramatic slave uprising in North America. He was born a slave in South Hampton County, Virginia, to Benjamin Turner and then sold to landowner Putnam Moore. Turner was always considered intelligent, extremely intelligent and literate for a slave, and was given to "visions" and "sightings" at an early age. He was very religious and became convinced that he was designated by God to lead a revolt that would free his people from the crushing brutality of slavery. On August 22, 1831, he and six other slaves began the revolt. Within forty-eight hours, he had accumulated an army of sixty. They moved across the countryside killing every white person they encountered. Although the group suffered no fatalities when attacked by the local militia, they became disorganized and only twenty rebels remained. During a subsequent attack, several were killed or captured. Nat Turner somehow managed to escape into the woods and was not found until September 30, 1831. He was imprisoned and while incarcerated dictated his socalled confessions. He was found guilty on November 5 and executed on November 11, along with sixteen other members of his army.

His revolt terrified southerners and helped to dispel the myth of the docile Negro slave. His name has since become an inspiration for black Americans to militate for their freedom no matter the cost.

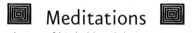 Meditations

(on the eve of his bold and daring enterprise)

When the lights come up, Nat Turner, age thirty-one, is standing center stage. He is short of stature.

Nat (Meditation 1):

I was looking at the men working in the fields today, cutting trees, building fences, moving rocks, picking fruit, planting vegetables, and tilling the soil. As I looked at them I tried to view them through the eyes of their masters, who see them as a subhuman species halfway between apes and humans on the evolutionary scale. Physically developed to do all the manual labor that comfort and ease Man but not mentally developed enough to be a part of the ruling class. And the proof they say is in the color of our skin. Black is the darkest part of night. Blackness is reputed to cover certain corners of hell. "The black man's destiny is to serve, and the white man's is to rule. That is God's plan and nothing on earth can change that. It was part of the master plan when the world was created."

I pondered this attitude and tried this experiment because I wanted to convince myself that this is so. Because if I can, it will make my life easier; I can put down this burden that I've been carrying around for so long and I can wake up each morning and go about my chores with peaceful compliance, bowing my head whenever Mr. Travis or his family passes my way. And do their bidding as requested of me no matter how arduous or menial. Mr. Travis is a kind master who places the greatest confidence in me. His wife and children are also kind people who try to obey the laws of God and live their lives according to the dictates of the Bible. I would like to love these people and devote my life to them. This is why I tried the experiment of seeing myself and others through their eyes. And I wish I had succeeded, but I haven't. I can't see myself as anything else than a superior example of God's creation. So therefore I must continue on the path that my mind has been leading me on for such a long while now.

The lights fade to black and soft music is heard. When the lights come up again, Nat is isolated in a spotlight on a different part of the stage.

Nat (Meditation 2):

Try as I can, and I have tried mightily, I cannot convince myself that I am an ordinary slave. The curious circumstances of my life and childhood are too unique. The signs and portents are too clear to be ignored.

When I was a child of three or maybe four years old I was relating in vivid detail the story of a cow that had wandered into a sinkhole and was up to his neck in the soft mud, about to be drowned, when a slave named Dewey, a large muscular man of great physical strength, passed by. Upon seeing the cow's dilemma, he fetched a rope, threw it around the cow's neck, and through a superhuman show of strength, he pulled that cow from the danger she was in.

On its face the story is remarkable. But what made it more remarkable was when my mother revealed that this incident had taken place more than ten years before I was born at a place quite far from here. So there was no way I could have heard about it or visualized it so vividly unless I was gifted with second sight. A divination that only God Almighty Master can bestow. It was then and there I determined that I would be a prophet. The Lord had shown me things that he keeps from others. The Lord had selected me to be his instrument here on earth. Even the master and his wife agreed that I was gifted in special ways. It was widely observed that a mind as restless, inquisitive, and observant as mine could never be in service to anyone as a slave. One example of this is how I learned how to read. I have no recollection of hearing of the alphabet or knowing anything about letters. But one day when a book was shown to me to keep me from crying, I began to spell the names of the different objects and pronounce the words correctly. This was without previous instruction or direction. Everyone was astonished, and I became the talk of the area for a short while.

As I grew older and thought about it more, I began to understand that God indeed had a special plan for me. What that plan was I had no idea. But I knew that through prayers and meditation it would one day be revealed to me. So it became my sacred duty to commune with my Maker as often as time allowed in order to discover my mission in life.

The stage goes dark once more. Then, again, Nat is spotlighted on a different part of the stage.

Nat (Meditation 3):

I had a dream one night and it was not a dream in the ordinary sense. It was truly a vision. I was asleep in the deepest part of the night when I felt a hand shaking me and a voice bidding me to wake up. I rose, looked around, but the room was empty. I was puzzled but not afraid. The temptation was to lay back down and to continue my sleep. I stood in the dark just wondering what it was that woke me in such an urgent fashion. And for no reason I went to the door, opened it, and ventured outside in the cool night air. A cloud was covering a half-moon in the sky and all around me was silence and darkness. Then the cloud passed and the moon was bright again. And over in the distance just beyond the trees, I saw images of men and women on horses. Upon closer view I could see that a fierce battle was taking place. But this was a battle without sound, only blood and butchery, and a fearsome show of anger and force. Black slaves were on one side, white masters on the other, and the battle raged on without abatement.

I have no idea how long I remained in that spot looking at this remarkable sight. It could have been an eternity or just an hour, I truly have no idea. But after a while another cloud moved and covered the moon once more. And when it passed the vision had passed with it. That sight has haunted me ever since I witnessed it, and not a night goes by that I don't dream about it. I've tried to understand and make sense of what I saw. And when I failed, I prayed. Prayed for wisdom and understanding and for true clarity of vision.

Lights dim, and then Nat is spotlighted on yet another part of the stage.

Nat (Meditation 4):

In 1825 a sudden urge to be alone came over me. I had been reading the New Testament about when Jesus went into the wilderness and fasted for forty days while being tempted by the devil. And it came to me that I must do the same. I must isolate myself in order for the Lord to truly enter my soul. So I ran away and remained in the woods for thirty days and nights, living off of herbs and pond water. And in spite of an extensive search with horses, dogs, and men I was not found. I could have eluded them indefinitely, but to the astonishment of everyone I returned after thirty days. "We thought you were gone forever," Wilson, one of the slaves on the farm said. "Thought you had gone East to someplace like New York or Canada." Then he added, "If it was me and I had escaped the way you done, they wouldn't see hide nor hair no more. No, sir." Others laughed behind my back, saying they thought I had some sense but now they find out that I don't. Even the new overseer looked at me in surprise when I walked back into the yard. He blinked twice, took off his hat, wiped his brow and said, "Well, I'll be."

Those folks are laughing but I had my reasons for returning, and it was not my business to tell them. But through depravation and meditation I achieved my ordination. I was now completely devoted to God. I had become His soldier and warrior here on earth. And like Joan of Arc before me I was destined to lead a bold and noble enterprise.

Lights dim, and then Nat is spotlighted on still another part of the stage.

Nat (Meditation 5):

The time is come and the signs are all in place. For three years I have waited for the Lord to send me a vision of revelation. During that time I have worshipped and preached his word to all who would listen. I have converted lost souls, baptized new converts, and preached the word of God far and wide. I also prayed for Him to show me when the time was right for me to begin. It came in two visions.

First I heard a loud noise in the heavens and the Spirit appeared to in the form of an angel. The angel said to me that the serpent was loose. That Jesus our Savior had laid down the yoke he had born for the sins of man. So that I could take it up and do battle with the serpent. The angel also said that the time was close at hand when the first would be last and the last would be first. And then he went away.

The second sign came shortly after that on a clear day in February. The sun shined brightly in the skies for hours and then changed colors several times. After that it grew dark and so did the world. Then all became bright again and everything was as it was before. Upon seeing this I fell to the ground with my face buried in the dirt. That is when I heard the voice ordering me to rise and prepare myself to slay my enemies, the people who have kidnapped and enslaved so many of God's beloved creations. It ordered me to slay them with their own weapons.

Pause.

Up until then I had kept the news of my revelations to myself. But now the time had come for me to share with others the great work that was laid out for me to do. And so I spoke to four men in whom I had great confidence. They immediately understood the great purpose of our holy enterprise and committed themselves to it completely. When I asked them why they wanted to fight, to a man they told me that their lives was worth nothing at all if they would have to be slaves for the rest of their time here on earth.

Our plans are now in place and all our preparations are made. Our time is at hand. Tomorrow is the day. In less than twelve hours a world that once was will be turned upside down and the destiny of a people will be altered forever. There can be no turning back. No doubt or hesitation. We must be resolute in our mission and execute it with dispatch. It is time for the future to begin.

Amen.

The lights go down. Again, another part of the stage is spotlighted, but it is empty. After a moment, the stage goes black.

OSCAR MICHEAUX
(1884–1951)

Oscar Micheaux was a determined filmmaker and an even more aggressive film entrepreneur. He started his company, the Micheaux Corporation, in 1918, first making short films and then quickly moving on to full-length features. In 1932, he released the first "all talking" motion picture made by a black film company; he then went on making movies—which he wrote, produced, directed, and released—for nearly thirty years. He was constantly besieged by financial troubles but survived in the film business through a combination of hustle, smarts, and a slight touch of knavery. He even gave Paul Robeson his first exposure in movies in the film *Body and Soul* (1925).

Today Micheaux is viewed as a pioneer whose films, though limited in technique and finesse, liberated blacks from the demeaning stereotypical roles given to them by Hollywood throughout the twenties, thirties, and forties.

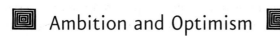 Ambition and Optimism

Oscar Micheaux, age forty-nine, a big, robust man with a very outgoing personality, is sprawled in an armchair, one foot over the arm, talking to a friend. He's wearing a flashy, double-breasted suit.

Oscar:

(*Laughing*) Most folks, especially ours, lack two things: optimism and ambition. The radio, the papers, and everywhere we look tells us things are bad, so we all walk around with our shoulders stooped and eyes down at our shoes. The world says, "You black, therefore you shouldn't have any ambitions or dreams." And we believe it. We become grateful for a job, work hard for small pay, and complain.

But we don't do anything about it. Yeah, sure, we organize some-times and join unions, but what does it get you in the end? A job, that's what it gets you. A job working for somebody else. Let me ask you a question. You know anybody who ever got rich working for somebody else? No, when you work, you makin' the boss rich, that's what you doin'. Not yourself, the boss. But most people don't seem to recognize that. Most people just so happy to be gettin' a regular paycheck every two weeks that they can't dream of nothin' else. But there's a lot of stuff out there, believe me and a lot of money too. All you have to do is go out there and look for it.

I been around this country more than a dozen times. Meet a lot of people, black, white, rich, poor, and a whole lot in between. All of them got some kinda money. A dollar or a hundred dollars. But all of it is money. That's the system we live in, capitalism. Capitalism mean money. Money for the big man, money for the little man, money for everybody in some kinda way if they want to go out and get it. Ain't no big trick to gettin' rich. But first the person has to have the optimism and the will to go after it. Optimism to dream that it is possible. Ambition to strategize a way to go out there and get it.

Pause.

When I started out in this motion picture business, everybody was telling me that the market was all sewed up. The big studios got it in a lock, and can't nobody, especially nobody colored, come in and cut in on that pie. So I ask about the Lincoln Company and some of the other small ones that I knew about. And they tell me that those companies are just limping along. (*Shaking his head, smiling*) People are always trying to discourage any undertaking that sound in any way ambitious. I don't know why that is, but that's the way people are. But I liked movies and liked the motion picture business and didn't see why I shouldn't try to get into it. The first try I made was when the Johnson boys wanted to buy my book *The Homesteader*, to make one of their photoplays out of it. I said sure, if they let me direct it. They said I didn't know anything about directing. They were right, I didn't. But I could learn, I told them. Other people were doing it, so how hard could it be? They laughed and told me no. So I told them goodbye and took my book with me.

That was the same thing that happened when I tried to get my first book published. These publishers gave me a whole lotta talk about editing and structure and syntax and point of view and all kinds of other things. When all I wanted to do was tell a story straight and simple as I like stories told to me. Then after all that talk and all those meetings they told me to forget it anyway. But I wasn't discouraged. I never get discouraged. If I did I'd be standing here in a uniform runnin' an elevator someplace, takin' my hat off to everybody that come in. But that ain't me, never was me. So what I did was investigate what this publishing business was all about. How books were put together and how much it cost to print them. After I found that stuff out, I asked everybody I knew to invest money in the publishing company I was going to start for publishing my book. I figured the worst they could say is no. But you'd be surprised how many said yes. So I got the book printed and bound.

Now the biggest part of printing a book is selling it. If you can't, you gonna end up with a warehouse full of books that nobody care about. The whole idea is to sell the book and recoup what you put in it plus something more. They call that marketing. I didn't know anything about that either. So I worked to find out. What I discovered was that none of the book dealers or sellers would touch my book. Said they only dealt with big established publishers and nobody else. So it meant that I had to find a way to do it on my own. That's what I mean when I say that you can't ever get discouraged. They put up obstacles and roadblocks in your way, and your job is to find a way around them.

A long time ago I heard a phrase that I have always found helpful. That phrase is, "Learn from the public, then take what they teach you, and use it to teach and sell them." A wise man told me that when I was a boy and it hasn't failed me yet. So what I did was filled up my car with boxes of book and drove all over the country knocking on doors, talking to people, and offering my book to buy. And in a little over ten months I sold out every copy I had. So I went back and had more printed. In ten years I sold thousands of copies of ten novels I wrote. I even design the covers for them too.

But I could see that the moving picture was the thing of the future. And a man always gotta look to the future if he wanna get ahead. The movies—"All Moving" . . . "All Brilliant" . . . "All

Spectacular" . . . and "All Glorious" too. Except for one thing. The way they portray us coloreds. Starting with *Birth of a Nation* and all the other stuff they been putting out lately. They always have us as some domestic or maid. Always lowdown or wild-eyed and stupid or criminal. What they don't realize or care about is, that stuff harms us as individuals and as a race. Now you and me know that the majority of us ain't like that, but the rest of the world don't. So they believe what they see. They believe those stereotypes. So I figure what we needed was movies that show the other side. Movies that show professional black people who are intelligent and experts at what they do. And that we have good-looking and sexy people in our race also. So it's movies like that I decided I would make.

Now I know for sure that there's a whole world of colored folks in this country waiting to see moving pictures like that. The reason I is so sure is because I am one of those people. The man who go to the movies and my taste ain't all that different. And I know how embarrassed I feel being portrayed as lowdown clowns and fools.

But I found out like I did with the publishing that I have to go out and learn what the moving picture business was all about. I also found out that it was harder. A whole lot harder because of all the technical and light things you have to do. It was also a whole lot more expensive too. Everything in movies cost money. From the camera to the film to the lighting to the actors to the processing house and the advertising. Everything, everything, is designed to break you if you don't know what you doin'. So once again I had to be hustling for money with my hat in hand and a big grin on my face. But where there's a will there's a way. And by hook and by crook I got *The Homesteader* made.

Then came the next obstacle, getting the managers and the owners to show it in their theatres. So once again I hit the road. This time instead of boxes of books I had cans of film in my car. The black theatre houses were a natural. But to make any money you gotta get your film into some of those white theatres too. So I made the circuit talking to white theatre owners and managers. They all looked at me like I was crazy. What white audience would be interested in seeing blacks where they ain't singing or dancing or making monkeyshines? But a few listened when I explained that they could get more black people coming to their theatre if they played something that black folks wanted to see. Now a lot of these people may be prejudiced, but a lot of them could also see past black and white. And what they saw was green. Money, the universal language. Capitalism again. So a lot of them book *The Homesteader* for midnight shows and special matinees and special shows just for colored audiences.

That first film of mine showed a five-thousand-dollar profit on a fifteen-thousand-dollar investment. Not bad. Not bad at all for a beginner. And what got me there? Optimism and ambition.

The coming of sound made things a lot harder and more expensive again. So I had to change my strategies and find a lotta shortcut ways for making my movies. But by this time I had already made more than fifteen films, all written, directed, and produced by me. So I had experience on how to do things on the run. I can't say it was easy, but I got them done.

The actors I used were a lotta help. No complaints, not even from the women. The minute I called they were ready. A lot of stuff we shot we could only do in one take with one lighting setup and no rehearsal time at all. But they were on top of it most of the time. When I was short on money to pay them they would let me slide until some came in, which was sometimes three to six months down the road. But we kept on going.

One of the things I started doing was looking close at the movies that the big theatres were playing that the big audiences were going to see. Then I would make a black version of the same kind of story. Because when it comes to going to pictures, people ain't all that different, black or white. They kind of all like the same things, more or less. And to survive in the movie business you better prepare to give the people what they want. So that's what I was doing. And that's what I'm always doing, giving the people what they want. You like gangster films? I'll make a gangster film. You like love stories? I'll make a love story. You like jungle pictures? I'll give you a jungle picture too. All with a different color and shade.

And we have stars too. Stars who are just as good as the ones in Hollywood. You like James Cagney, I'll give you a Cagney, only this one is darker and got more soul. I got me a black Valentino, a sepia Mae West, a bronze Mary Pickford, and a dusky Joan Crawford. All of them talented, all of them wonderful. And like the studios I'll even send them out on tour to promote their films.

So, see, what I'm saying is it's all a matter of optimism and ambition. And of course having fun while you're doing it. Man, if it ain't fun there's just no point in doing it. I've been in this movie business for fifteen years and although it ain't always been heaven, it's never been hell. And I wouldn't give up any of it for anything else. And I hope to go on for another fifteen years and another fifteen and another fifteen until I'm so old that I can't look through a camera anymore. That's how much fun I've been having. But I still go back to the same old thing: ambition and optimism . . . optimism and ambition . . . and a good sense of humor too. That's all it takes.

PAUL ROBESON
(1898–1976)

Singer, actor, activist Paul Robeson, the son of a slave who escaped to freedom at age fifteen, was born in Princeton, New Jersey, and educated at Rutgers University in 1919, where he earned a Bachelor of Arts degree. He was also an honors student, a twelve-letter athlete, and a football all-American. At Columbia University he became the third black graduate of its Law School. After a brief period at a prestigious law firm, Robeson focused his attention on acting. He had appeared in several theatre productions in college and attracted the attention of playwright Eugene O'Neill, who offered him the leading role in his play *The Emperor Jones*. Robeson refused the role but accepted a part in O'Neill's *Taboo*. In 1925, he did join the cast of *The Emperor Jones* and later starred in the film as well. In this play he had occasion to sing, and this brought him considerable critical praise and a new career as a singer. He gave his first concert that year and toured the United States as well as Europe several years after that. He also acted in many motion pictures and Broadway plays, including a celebrated version of Shakespeare's *Othello* in the 1940s.

His political beliefs led him to speak out against the injustices African Americans were suffering in this country. He made several trips to Russia to play concerts and accept awards. During the war, he spoke out against the Nazis, and his concerts were popular all over Europe. After the war, he spoke out more vociferously against the injustice that the poor and oppressed of the world were experiencing. In America, he challenged government agencies to do better by African Americans. Because of this, he was labeled a Communist and denied a passport to travel. The U.S. government made a considerable effort to discredit and silence him, but Robeson stood up to all of it, never backing down for a moment. In 1958, he published a book entitled *Here I Stand*. He retired from his active stage career in 1963.

During his prime, Robeson was a popular stage and screen actor, an accomplished singer, and a symbol of the artist as social activist. Today he is viewed as a genuine American hero.

Paul Robeson, in his early fifties, stands before the House Un-American Activities Committee (HUAC).

Robeson:

I invoke the Fifth Amendment.

I am here before the House Un-American Activities Committee because I have exercised my right as an American citizen to speak out for the rights of the suppressed and exploited black people of this nation. My fellow Negroes here in the United States. To me that is not un-American, it is very American, it is a right guaranteed to us by the Constitution, the foundation on which this nation was formed. It is this committee that is un-American and I refuse to be persecuted by it. So therefore I invoke the Fifth Amendment.

My name is Paul Robeson and anything I have to say that is critical of the way black people in this country are treated I have said in public. That is why I am here. I was born and bred an American and I love it. I love a part of it, but what I don't love is what it has done and continues to do to me and the people of African origins who have worked hard to make this country what it is. My father was a slave and my people died to build this country. Yet now we are being persecuted, vilified, and treated like second-, third-, and tenth-class citizens. I refuse to witness this in silence, so wherever I go, whatever public stage I am granted, I speak out. I speak out loudly against it. And that is the reason I am called here before this body. I invoke the Fifth Amendment. The Fifth Amendment does not infer criminality. The Supreme Court is very clear on this point.

I am here because the State Department, who revoked my passport and refused my many efforts to acquire a new one, says that I should not be allowed to travel because I have struggled and used my celebrity in an attempt to gain independence for the suppressed colonial peoples of Africa. I am very proud of that fact.

I am here because in 1946 I visited the White House and appealed to Harry S. Truman in his capacity as president of the United States to do something about the many lynchings of people of color in the South. I said to him, and I told him very clearly, that if the government did not do something about this horrible condition that we Negroes would. He asked me if that was a threat. I told him no. I said it was merely a statement of fact about the mood and temper of our people in the face of this brutal injustice. I likened the current lynchings to the Nazi war crimes and the Nuremburg trials. The president could not appreciate the analogy. He told me that loyal Americans should not mix domestic problems like lynching with foreign policies. He also said that government actions against lynchings were a political matter and that the timing of any action was an important consideration. I found myself wondering how the black men and women who were dragged out by masked hoodlums carrying the burning cross and strung up on trees would have felt about this remark. Furthermore, I found myself wondering if Mr. Truman would have made such a remark if he or any member of his family had been subjected to such treatment. When the government chooses to stand mute in the face of such injustices, it is incumbent on its citizens to speak out. And it is for that reason that I have been brought here.

I am here because I refuse to allow the government and the society of this country to use my so-called success and the success of a few other Negroes as an example of the prosperity that all our black citizens share. This is simply not so. Several thousands of black folks in the South live on merely seven hundred dollars a year. And there are reports from various universities that verify this fact. America should be ashamed of itself. I say it loud and I'll keep on saying it till these conditions change.

I am called before this committee because I went to Russia and was given medals for singing and for peace. What is not acknowledged or noted by this committee is that I have also received medals and citations from the Abraham Lincoln High School and from many other parts of the world on behalf of persecuted people.

I am here because in Paris several thousand students who came to hear me sing and who represented six or seven hundred million people of various ethnic backgrounds requested that I say on their behalf that they did not want war.

I belong to the spirit of American resistance, which fights against any kind of imperialism, including American imperialism. For this I am called un-American. In the newspapers they are saying all kinds of derogatory things about me. They are calling me dangerous. They are calling me the enemy and a traitor to the land of my birth. But I believe if Frederick Douglass or Harriet Tubman was standing here they would be called all those names too. So I am not ashamed, I am not embarrassed, and I will not be cowed.

I am not in any conspiracy against this country and never have been. It should be plain to everybody, especially to my fellow blacks, but if the government or this committee had any evidence to back up their charges they would not only put me in jail but under it. This committee is a joke and an embarrassment to the principles that this country stands for. It should be adjourned. It should be adjourned forever.

"QUEEN" MARY
(?)

"Queen" Mary was a fiery and outspoken woman who worked alongside Buddoe in organizing the slave uprising in the Virgin Islands. In temperament she was the complete opposite of Buddoe. Where he was reflective and somewhat introspective, she was instinctive and outspoken, given more to action than to compromise. Like "General" Buddoe no one knows what became of her after the proclamation of freedom was announced. But her leadership abilities during the uprising and the way her oratory could move and inspire a crowd became the stuff of legend. There are many songs, calypsos mostly, praising her and her firebrand personality.

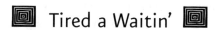 Tired a Waitin'

"Queen" Mary, a woman warrior in her mid-forties, strong, psychic, fiery in speech and manner, is talking to a group of slaves.

Mary:

Fire's a tool, fire's a weapon. Fire's a sign from heaven that can turn this island into a hell if we don' get what we want tonight. The night is dark as you can see, and the moon is hidin' he face because he don' want to see what he might have to look at tonight. Because from where he is right now if the moon lookin' down, what he got to see on this island is thousands and thousands a flambeaux lightin' up the night, everyone lookin' like some kind of eye of God. These flambeaux in the air right now but they ain' gonna be there long if we don' get what we want. They gone be on the ground lightin' up the world, spreading hell and damnation for every Danish man, woman, and child livin' here. And for any other person free or unfree who is fool enough to side with 'em. That's what the moon will see because that's what's goin' to be if we don' get what we want.

I tired a talkin' to 'em. I tired a listenin' to 'em too. Them people ain' never sayin' anything new. It's always, "Wait . . . have patience . . . soon . . . trust in the Lord and he will deliver you." But you and I know, soon is a day that will never come as far as these people is concerned. And when they say, "The Lord will provide," they mean he gon' provide for them and not for us. He is their god that's smilin' down on them and peein' on us. Because if he wasn't we wouldn't be slaves in the first place.

We got our own gods. Black gods. I talk to them and they tell me that if we want anythin' done we have to do it ourselfs. I is a woman who bear nine different children from four different men. Why? Because the Massa tell me I have to. And I didn't even get to bring any of my own children up except for one. All they ever done is let me nurse them and teach them how to walk. And then they take them away from me, to sell to somebody so the Massa could get rich.

I is a woman who worked day and night till I could barely stand. Just because some frowsy white bitch woman say that I had to.

I is a woman who had to bed down with men I didn't like. I is a woman who had to bed down with the Massa when his milk-white wife was sick or not in the mood to do her wifely duties. And I is a woman that same Massa beat because his wife tell him to do so when she find out what he is doing with me. So what I sayin' is that I want to see all the white people on this island dead like yesterday fish. And I is ready to do that if they don' do what it is we want 'em to do.

You got to be really rough with these people because they been rough with us all our lives. They never see us as people like them, flesh and blood and brains. They only see us as animals whose only job is to work hard, serve them, give them pleasure, and then die. So our business is to make them see who we is once and for all. And if they don', send them all to the fires of hell where they belong.

Buddoe want to talk to them. He want to negotiate. I ain' for that. I say we burn 'em and we burn 'em now. I say we pull 'em out their house like they do to us, tie 'em to the whippin' post, and whip 'em so they can feel what it like. I want them to know that their bullets don't frighten us no more. We been shot too much, whip too much, cut too much, and kicked too much. So now it's our turn. We already burn down the Counting House and we burn down the Deed House. So now all the records is gone about who own who. We done burn a lot of stuff already, but the one thing we ain' burn yet is the white man. Buddoe say wait and I plan to wait. But I ain' waitin' too long, because like you, I is damn tired a waitin'.

RALPH JOHNSON BUNCHE
(1905–1971)

Political scientist, educator, government diplomat, the first African American to win the Nobel Prize, Ralph Johnson Bunche was one of the most prominent Americans of his generation. He taught at Harvard and worked for the U.S. State Department, where he distinguished himself as a statesman and diplomat. Later he became the director of the Department of Trusteeship and Non-Self Governing Territories at the United Nations. In 1948 he led a peace-seeking endeavor that brought about an agreement for peace in the Arab/Israel conflict. For this he was awarded the Nobel Prize for Peace. Other awards include the NAACP Award in 1949 and the Presidential Medal for Freedom in 1963. He retired from the United Nations in 1971.

 A New World Order

(a prayer)

Ralph Bunche, a man of forty-four, enters the stage, waits a moment, and then kneels as if in prayer.

Bunche:

Dear God, holy father in heaven, if you exist. . . . No I can't do this. (*He rises*) I can't kneel, even in prayer, because I don't believe that any human need supplicate himself in such a fashion in order to talk to the supreme maker of us all. If you do exist. If there's really a God up there in the sky, or wherever it is people say you reside.

My relationship with you, as you well know, has always been problematical. According to the time of day, the mood I'm in, the season on the calendar, or state of my emotional barometer, I have either believed in you or haven't.

Practical reason says you don't exist. And if you do, why would the problems of one anonymous person like myself be worthy of commanding your attention or interest? On the other hand, a certain kind of intellectual conceit tells me that there is more to life than the things that we can see, taste, or touch. That there is a spiritual sphere that we must acknowledge and actively communicate with if we are to function fully and dimensionally as human beings.

It has been said and often repeated that if God didn't exist, man would have to create him. And in so doing he would create him in his own image and likeness. And perhaps that's what I'm doing. Creating you in my own image and likeness. If this is so, that is the reason I'm not kneeling. Because I cannot conceive of anyone kneeling to me. And I cannot believe that any God of any design or configuration would require that of anyone either.

There is no reason that you should respond or listen to anything I say, because I am a convenient parishioner. I call on you when I am in need and forget or even deny your existence when I am not. But if you are as benevolent a deity as I am led to believe, perhaps you will ignore this flaw in my character. Anyway here goes.

Our leader on this mission has just been killed and I am assigned to carry on his work. I embrace the task with great fervor, especially in the face of the great sacrifices that have already been made on the mission's behalf. I will devote all the energy I have, both physical and intellectual, to the peaceful resolution of this terrible conflict between the Arabs and Jews that is challenging the notion of peace and stability in that region. But in order to go into this battle and attempt to achieve some sort of change for the better I must be clear on what it is I am after. And what it is I believe.

I came from the U.S. State Department to the United Nations in the firm belief that this organization is the greatest instrument devised by man for keeping and ensuring peace on our planet. François Voltaire said that "war is the greatest of all crimes" and that it should be avoided at all costs. Because the price of war is death, destruction, and human degradation of all kinds. There are no real victors in armed conflict, only victims on both sides. If we need proof of this we only have to look at the end result of the so-called Great War we have just been through. Much of Europe, Asia, and other parts of our globe was destroyed. Economies shattered and families the world over are still mourning the loss of dear and beloved members of their tribe or clan.

It is easy for us to say, "We need to make the world safe for this or that," and I admit that the cause is often just and righteous. And I am aware that there are people in the world, leaders of countries, who cannot be talked to or reasoned with. Whose aggression knows no bounds. Whose arbitrary need for causing pain and suffering in others can only be curtailed by the show of military might and force. But I see that as a last resort. An extreme measure that should only be enacted when all else has failed.

You see, Lord, I believe, I must believe, that all men, most men, are reasonable, intelligent, and desirous of peace. Not only for themselves and their families but for their friends and acquaintances as well.

I believe that the problems of nations are human problems. And that human problems can always be resolved by both sides sitting down, laying their agendas on the table, listening to each other, and coming to a peaceful resolution through compromise and honest integrity.

In the recorded history of our civilization there has been a long succession of imperialism, suppression, and exploitation that must be acknowledged and then overcome if we are to achieve the peace and harmony we all so fervently desire. Our addiction to concepts and attitudes of narrow nationalism (or patriotism), racial and religious persecution, along with our overwhelming lust for material things at the expense of the dignity and spiritual well-being of others, must be contained, modified, or stopped. This I believe must be accomplished in one way or another if we are to move forward as a society or a civilization.

I work for the United Nations. And in this small instance, Lord, I am the United Nations. I, along with my colleagues on this mission, represent what the U.N. stands for. Therefore the face we present must necessarily be the face of this august body. Which is why I need to be clear on what it is I believe.

I believe that peace among nations can be achieved and sustained over a long period of time. But it cannot be achieved in a vacuum. It must be achieved by an enlightened and expanded view of the human condition all over the world. By the acknowledgment that all people, irrespective of race, religion, or political ideology, must be respected, listened to, and valued as being equal in any discussion or negotiation. This approach to world affairs I believe can lead to freedom, peace, and a better life for all men.

This prayer is easy to come by. Pessimism is easy to embrace. But optimism and hope take courage and tenacity. They also take a committed will to move forward when all the signposts are saying turn back. But to turn back represents a retreat into a darker time that we have hopefully put behind us.

My fear, my big fear, is that I'm not up to the task that I have been trusted with. That I will fail. That I will bend when I should stand firm, that I will break when I should be flexible. So I come to you in prayer seeking the strength I don't think I possess. Hoping that you, for this short period, will endow me with the stamina and fortitude I will need for this undertaking. And that I will see it through in a way that will make this organization proud and prove to the world the validity of the United Nations as an instrument for keeping the peace.

I have this dream of a new world order, where now and in the future all disputing nations will expose their differences to the peaceful efforts of the United Nations. It is the only way I can see that truth, justice, and reason can prevail.

ROSA PARKS
(1913–2005)

Rosa Parks stood up, figuratively speaking, by refusing to stand. By refusing to stand and yield her seat to a white bus passenger on a bus in Montgomery, Alabama, in 1965, she stood up to the oppressive segregation laws in the South. Her act of refusal and subsequent arrest became the spark that ignited the historic Montgomery Bus Boycott, which became the first important victory in the African American fight for equality in the United States. Ms. Parks remained an activist for civil rights throughout her life, and in 1996 was awarded the Presidential Medal of Freedom by President Clinton. Today she is generally regarded and affectionately called the "Mother of the Civil Rights Movement."

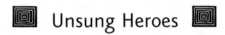 **Unsung Heroes**

Eight years after the Montgomery bus boycott Rosa Parks is talking informally to a group of people. She is seated on a chair and remains seated throughout.

Rosa:

Every time I'm invited to talk to groups such as this, whether they are large or small, it's always to recount the events of my arrest that led to the Montgomery bus boycott. This will probably go down as the most significant event in my life and perhaps accurately so. Still, there are times when my mind and my memory would like to dwell on other things, people, and events. So if you will indulge me this time, I will be very grateful.

Pause.

There is an old saying that goes, "Behind every great man there is a great woman." I would like to turn that statement around and say, "Often behind every great woman there is a great man." Not that I think that I am great or that anything I've done is great. Far from it. It's just that I would like to indicate that among our people, there are many great men whose strength, dedication, and heroism go unheralded for a variety of reasons. I know in my case this is true. And the hero I'm talking about is Raymond Parks, son of the carpenter David Parks and his wife Geri Culbertson Parks. We've been married now for more than thirty years, and there isn't a day that goes by or endeavor that I undertake that I don't draw from his strength, his steadfastness, and his knowledge.

From the first time we met, during the Depression, he was talking and showing me examples of the injustices in this country perpetrated against people with darker skin. The funny thing is that our meeting isn't as one would think. I was eighteen, quiet, and very devoted to the St. Paul African Methodist Episcopal Church. During the day I was earning my keep, mostly by cleaning people's houses and doing a little sewing on the side. Through my friend Essie, I met this man Raymond Parks. He was a sharp dresser, full of smiles and talk, and very handsome too. But I didn't like him. I didn't like him at all. I didn't like him for one reason. He was light skinned. Very light skinned. So light skinned that people sometimes mistook him for white. I had this thing about light-skinned black folks at the time. I didn't like them, because I thought they were always trying to pass. That they were ashamed of their heritage and thought themselves better than dark-skinned black folks. But Lord was I wrong about Raymond on that count. But I didn't know it at the time, so I was very standoffish with him. In fact, if I remember rightly, I hardly spoke to him at all. Still it was clear that he was trying to make an impression on me, just from the way he was talking and from the way that he was eyeing me up and down.

The other strike against him was his age. He was twenty-eight, ten years older than me. And in my mind at the time twenty-eight seemed on the edge of being ancient. I didn't want to be going out with an old man, so that was that.

But whatever resistance I put up, however indifferently I acted, it didn't seem to matter to him. The man was persistent, I'll give him that. He would ask me out time after time on dates. And time after time I would simply tell him no. But for some reason the man never would get discouraged. He just kept on trying and trying until one day I couldn't say no anymore, so I said yes.

It was on that first date I got a glimpse of what he was like and how proud he was of his race. He was also proud about all the things that black people were doing and achieving. And not just here in America, but all over the world. Raymond worked as a barber and always made sure that the barbershop had copies of all the better-known black newspapers and magazines. He was also a charter member of the Montgomery branch of the NAACP. As we walked in the park and went out to dinner afterward I remember thinking to myself, "This man is a whole lot different than what I thought, and a whole lot different from the men I know." So different in fact that you know what he did on our second date? (*Quick pause*) He asked me to marry him.

When I told him I didn't think we knew each other well enough, know what he said? "That ain't no obstacle. We will get to know each other over the years after we are married." Being the kind of person that I am, I didn't let that sway me. We went together for over a year, and in December 1932 we got married.

It was during that same time that I began to become more aware of what was going on and happening to black people in this country. Especially in the South. No, that isn't quite right. I was always aware, but I wasn't always active. Not in any big way. I mean I would send money to groups, sign petitions, and things like that. But with Raymond, I started to truly get involved. You see, he wasn't somebody who just sat around talking about what a shame it was what they are doing to us in the various southern states. He was always getting groups together, going to meetings, or initiating meetings himself to plan strategies on how they could fight what was going on. When you are around somebody like that who you love and admire, it's hard not to get involved yourself.

And as I said before, he was always reading about blacks and their achievement, whether it was in sports, politics, or art. I can't tell you how many times he would read and recite sections from James Weldon Johnson's *God's Trombones,* pointing out to me how powerful it was and how beautiful too. "People like to talk about

Shakespeare and stuff," he would say. "But to me this is just as good or maybe even better."

When the bus incident occurred all those years later, he was the first one there to see that I was all right. To see that I wasn't hurt in any kind of way. Then when the boycott began, and Martin and the rest put so much effort behind it, he said to me, "Rose, you know I'm proud of you and what you're doing. But I'm worried too. I don't want you to become a target for some crazy white person who will try to make you some kind of martyr to this cause. So I want you to think real careful about how much you want to be involved with this thing."

I told him I knew about the danger and it wasn't just to me. It was to everybody involved with the movement. "Yes, but you see I'm not married to everybody, I'm married to you." I assured him over and over again that I would be fine. So finally he said, "All right I can respect that. But you have to understand I am always going to be worried."

As time went by my name got more and more in the papers. People in groups were always asking me to come to their gatherings or rallies to make speeches or to meet other people. I noticed that Raymond was starting to shrink more and more in the background. Some folks went so far as to suggest that he was jealous of all the attention I was getting. But that wasn't so. You see, he kept up with everything that was going on in the civil rights movement and would discuss it with me in detail at home. He would also listen to any talk I was going to give and made suggestions on ways to improve it or make it more interesting. The reason I think he was pulling more and more into the background is that he was shy. It was something I hadn't noticed before, because he wasn't that way in the barbershop, at home, or among friends. But in places where large crowds would gather he always seemed to want to maintain his anonymity. Several times at public meetings I would ask him to sit on the stage with me. His answer was always the same. "Those people didn't come to see or hear me. They are here for you. I'll be where you can see me, have no fear." Then he would smile, pour himself a drink, and take a sip. He likes gin. Likes it a little bit too much sometimes, if you ask me. And when I mention it to him, know what he would say? "You know, you're right about that, Rose.

Absolutely right." Then he would go on and take another sip anyway.

I'm telling you this because I don't want you to think that he is any kind of saint. Raymond got his faults like everybody else, including me. But what I guess I'm saying is that those faults were nothing compared to his strengths. And without those strengths I wouldn't be where I've been or done any of the things I've done.

I've been hearing talk in many different places where people, especially women, are talking their man down. Saying black men ain't this, black men ain't that. They don't know how to respect women and don't seem to find beauty in their own. Some are saying it because they've had bad experiences. Other are saying it I suppose because they think that it's cool or the thing to do. Well, I don't like it. And sometimes I even get upset when I hear it. I say before we rush to make judgments, we should ask ourselves what fires it is that these men have been through and look at the quiet way they hold it in most of the time, because when you do that what you are looking at is a character that is stronger than steel.

Raymond Parks is my unsung hero. There are many out there; recognize them, please.

ST. MARTIN DE PORRES
(1579–1639)

St. Martin de Porres was born in Lima, Peru, shortly after the city was founded. His father was a Spanish gentleman who later became the governor of Panama. His mother was a black freedwoman. As a boy Martin apprenticed as a barber and as a physician. At age fifteen he entered the Dominican order and some years later was ordained a lay brother. Throughout his life he devoted himself wholeheartedly to the poor and the sick. His compassion and generosity was extended to animals of every kind as well. Because of his extreme spirituality he was said to possess wondrous abilities, which many called miracles, such as healing the sick and being able to feed many with a small amount of food. It was said he had the ability to suspend himself in the air and put himself in many places at the same time. He was also known far and wide for the warmth of his personality and for his ability to calm the most tortured spirit. He died in 1639, and was canonized a Catholic saint in 1962. Today he is known as the "Apostle of Charity" and the father of the sick, the poor, and the helpless.

 I Am Blessed

Martin, age twenty-four, is dressed in the plain brown vestment of the Dominican order. His garment is clean but tattered. He is seated, speaking to a small group of people. His personality and manner is genial, soft-spoken, and kindly.

Martin:

Blessed is the soul who finds his direction early in life. I was one of the lucky ones. I discovered my vocation when I was fifteen years old. I was walking through the plaza on my way from the marketplace where my mother had sent me to purchase a hen and some vegetables for our supper. It was to be a celebration for a visitor who was coming to the small house where my sister and I lived with our mother. I was given very specific instruction of the kind of hen to buy and how it should be butchered for cooking. And this was also true with the vegetables. I did as I was told and was attentive to every detail. Now I was walking home in triumph because I had accomplished my mission. Mother would be pleased.

But as I crossed through the plaza my eye caught the face of a sick old man sitting on a bench, begging for alms. And I thought to myself, "What good will money do for this old man who is so sick?" So I asked him the question and he replied, "Money will give me the means to buy food and restore my strength. Then I will be healthy again." But as I looked at him I could tell that food alone would not restore his health. He needed the spiritual nourishment that only prayer and meditation could provide. When I told him so, he cursed and spit at me. Said I was a fool and a miscreant. Said that prayers were only words wasted and thrown in the air. That food was the substance of health and money the means to prosperity. In spite of his anger I kneeled right there in the plaza and quietly prayed for him while he shouted for me to stop and leave him alone. When I finished praying I rose and left.

But before leaving the plaza I encountered a woman with a small child whose hungry eyes beseeched me in such a way that I stopped and went over to them. The baby cried but the woman said nothing. But I could see from the look on her face and the agony in her eyes that she was starving. Starving in such a way that the pain was unimaginable. Immediately I gave her the vegetables and the hen for her to cook to feed her child and herself. I somehow knew that this was the right thing to do. We must always help those less fortunate than us. I was just a boy, but I knew that my mission in life was to help and give comfort to those in need no matter the cost.

While I was doing this there was a man watching me. This man was dressed in the splendid finery of a knight. Handsome and magnificent, he sat majestically on a splendid-looking horse.

When I got home and told my mother what I had done, she shouted at me for my stupidity, then cried in despair because she had nothing to feed our guest when he arrived. I didn't know what to tell her except that I was sorry. But I wasn't. In my heart I knew that what I had done was right.

Our guest arrived. He was the handsome knight that I saw at the plaza. Mother introduced him as my father, who for personal reasons had to leave right after my sister was born. He told her what he saw me do in the plaza and said that I should be praised, not scolded, for my generosity. Then he produced several gold coins and sent out for all sorts of food for us to eat.

The following day in the plaza I prayed for the sick old man again, and he cursed me again. And day after day, for more than two weeks, I went to the plaza, where I prayed for him. Then one day he did a strange thing. He stopped swearing and spitting at me and began to join me in prayer. In less than three days the sores that covered him so badly began to leave his body. Soon after this his eyes became bright and clear and his body upright instead of the bent over position as it had been for so long. In less than a week he had regained his health, just through the power of prayers. He and others called it a miracle. I called it a sign from God that helping the sick and poor was my calling.

Shortly after I journeyed to the Dominican friary and asked if I could join as a servant to sweep their floors and clean their laundry. They asked if I was sincere, and I told them they could test me. I was allowed to live there and work for a month as a trial. Afterward I was invited to stay as long as I liked.

Now, although I had apprenticed as a physician and a barber, I wanted the lowliest job to humble myself in the eyes of God and my fellowman. But soon I was pressed into cutting the hair of all the friars and working with the sick. My father, I am told, was pleased when he heard that I was at the Dominican monastery. But when he heard in what capacity, he said that I was just wasting my family name. He was at the time governor of Panama and in that capacity sent a message to our prior requesting that I be made a priest. The prior tried to oblige, but I refused. I was not worthy, I explained to him. I was doing exactly as God wanted me and no other person, including the governor of Panama, should be able to change that. Beside which I knew that my father was only upset because of his pride. But who could respect a man who had left his offspring and their mother because she was "Negrittra" and he was a Spanish grandee with Castilian blood?

So I went on with my work at the monastery, helping the sick and the poor of the area. And in this capacity I was able to perform many deeds on their behalf that people said were miraculous. But to me it was just God manifesting His compassion and generosity through me.

Yesterday, on my twenty-fourth birthday, I was accepted into the Dominican order as a lay brother. It was the happiest day of my life. Now I can continue doing the work of God until he calls me to His side. I believe that a man should ask no more of himself than to do God's will and accomplish God's destiny for him. I have come this far and now it is time to continue. I am blessed as you can see, because God has touched me so kindly.

SOJOURNER TRUTH
(1797–1883)

Sojourner Truth's real name was Isabella Baumfree. She was born a slave in New York City, became deeply religious at an early age, and sought her freedom by running away several times before the New York State Emancipation Act of 1827 freed all slaves in the state. In 1843, as a result of a religious vision, she changed her name to Sojourner Truth and traveled to rallies on abolition throughout the United States. Although she couldn't read or write, she became the first black woman to speak out publicly against slavery. After the Civil War she championed equal treatment for blacks in all areas, especially education. She was also a champion of women's rights, and gave her famous "Ain't I a Woman" speech at a National Suffrage Convention in Akron, Ohio, in 1852.

 ## The Power of Words: Starting to Learn

Isabella Baumfree (Belle), age thirty-one, has not yet evolved into the dynamic and powerful creature known as Sojourner Truth that she will become fifteen years later. She is just a young woman starting to discover her voice and perhaps her destiny.

Belle:

I been learnin' new words and what they mean. Every day for a while now. The good people I been workin' for and the blessed people who been helpin' me through this court case been usin' so many different words and sayin' them so fast that for a while I wasn't even sure that it was English they was talkin'. It might a been some language that was close to English but with a whole lotta different words. But of course I knowed better than that even when I was thinkin' it. I knowed that the truth is I was ignorant about the way educated people talk and the educated words they like to use.

141

See, you gotta remember that I was a slave until I left over a year ago and none of the five masters that owned me, including Mr. Dumont, the nicest one of the bunch, ever teach me anything about book learnin'. So I come this far and got this old without really knowing how educated people converse with each other. But like I said, that is changin' day by day. I still don't know how to read, but that'll be the next thing comin', God willin'.

The whole uproar was of course about my son Peter and whether or not I was goin' to get him back after them Geaney people sold him to that Southern farmer Fowler that their daughter had married. And now that man he up and take my little Peter, six years old and as innocent as one of God's angels, down to Alabama, where if I don't take a hand he gon' grow up in slavery for sure. So whether they like it or not I'm goin' to fight for my child. And that's the long and short of it.

I was sixteen years old and didn't have too much a care in the world except for doin' what I was told so I didn't get a beatin'. Master Dumont and his wife was my owners at the time, and she could be as mean as a skunk when she was ready. But he would stop her from hittin' me, sayin' to her, "Belle is the hardest working colored I know. She can do the work of half a dozen like her and still come in for more. A slave like that you shouldn't beat too much. A slave like that you gotta feed and keep her strong. She can mean real money in your pocket one day."

Because I worked so hard the other slaves didn't like me, call me all kinds of names. But I didn't care. If it would save me from a beatin' or get me something extra to eat, I would work all day and all night if they asked me. So for that time everything was all right. I even got the chance, when it was Pentecost season for the white folks, to go to the Pinkster Carnival, where us colored, free ones and slaves, could get together with music and food, dance, sing, and talk about Africa. I love to dance and love to hear the stories I was being told. Love to see the costumes some people were dressed up in. For this carnival we also had a king. Black King Charles. He would wear a crown and walk around smilin' at everybody with a cape and a rod in his hands.

It was the last night of our celebration when I saw this boy standin' across the way talkin' to some people. And just as I looked at him he looked over at me and our eyes kind of meet. And it was like there was no one else in the place but us. My heart went over to him and his came over to me. We start to talk and then dance. Later on we went for a walk in the night just holdin' each other's hands. He told me his name was Robert and the farm he belonged too. I told him my name and then we kissed. After that we walked some more looking for a place we could lie together and be alone in the moonlight. When we got back he said, "I love you." I told him that I loved him too. After that night he would sneak up to the Dumont farm whenever he could, and when he arrived, which was always in the night, he would find me there waitin'.

We was in love and there was no secret. Mr. Dumont knowed about it and didn't seem to mind. But when Robert's owner Mr. Catlin found out he went kinda crazy. "What if she has a baby from Robert? The Dumonts will own it and I will get nothing from all the money I spent on that boy," he said. And forbid Robert from ever seein' me again. But Robert wouldn't obey and kept on comin' to visit till Mr. Catlin found out and beat him so bad that Robert could hardly walk anymore. After that Robert never come again.

"It's time you were married and made us some babies." Mr. Dumont said to me one day. "I picked out a nice man for you to marry, his name is Thomas and he'll be a good husband to you I'm sure." I knowed the Thomas he was talkin' about and tried to remember what he was like. The first thing that come to mind is that he was old. More than twice my age and his hair was turnin' gray too. He had been married before and had got children who had all been sold away.

When we meet up, the man had a tired look on his face. His body was thin and bent like he had worked too hard for too long for most of his life. He was nothin' like Robert but there was nothin' I could do. Mr. Dumont had picked him for me and I had to obey. "I hope you don't mind," Thomas said to me. "I'll be good to you and treat you with respect." I could see he was a good man and he mean what he was sayin'. My problem was that I didn't love him. And I never could no matter how long we would stay married. I didn't say that to him but I could see from his face that he knew it. But still in all we had to marry because Mr. Dumont said it.

My first child was born in a little shack on the Dumont proper-ty. We called her Diana after my sister. My next child was Thomas, a loud-crying boy. Mr. Dumont was happy because masters prefer boys to girls. They was worth more when you sold them. Then when little Thomas took sick and died Dumont got angry. "I'm losing my investment, losing the money I invest," he said. And nothing more.

The next child I has was a boy too. We called him Peter. Then we had a girl, we called her Lizzie. Thomas never said much, and never did much except work hard all day and keep his head down whenever anybody was talkin' to him. And in spite of all the children we was givin' birth to, we didn't have much of anything in common.

Then out of the blue came the announcement: *all slaves born before Independence Day 1799 are going to be free in one year.* This was the new law in New York, and all the slaves was talkin' about it, even Thomas. "We gon' be free," he kept sayin'. "We gon' be free."

Mr. Dumont wasn't happy about this law, but there wasn't nothin' he could do except obey. But I gotta say that man work me and work me and work me some more. It was like he was tryin' to get a lifetime of work out of me in the one year he had left. When I couldn't take it no more I decided to run away. It was three months before the state law said we was free. And I coulda got into real trouble if I was caught, but I didn't care. I just had to go. So I picked up my little daughter Sophie and started to walk. I didn't look back, I just kept on walkin' forward hoping that nobody would be comin' for me and my child. Ten miles down the road I come up on the house of Mr. Isaac Van Wagenen and his wife, Maria. These were churchgoing people I knew to be against slavery. When I told them what I done, they took Sophie and me in and told us we could live there. When Mr. Dumont found out he was boilin' mad. He came to the house and demanded that I come back. "I own you, you are my property," he said. "You and your child." I told him I didn't care what he had to say, that the law of God said that no man is supposed to own another human person. But the way slavery have it you can. So I'm sayin' to you, Mr. Dumont, you can take me back to your farm, but I'm gonna keep leavin' and leavin' until I is either free or dead.

I guess he heard what I said and knowed that I meant it, because he let Mr. Van Wagenen and his wife buy me for twenty dollars and Sophie for five dollars. Then as soon as they did, they told me I was free.

When the day of freedom finally arrived, July 4, 1827, there was singin' and rejoicin' everywhere. It was like a miracle none of us ever thought we would witness in our lifetime but here we was as free as any bird in the sky. Then after our songs of freedom died down I begun to wonder about my children. Accordin' to the law they were still goin' to be slaves for a lot more years. I was also worried about their safety so I went to inquire about them. That's when I found out that Peter had been sold to that man Fowler who had took him down South. Diana and Elizabeth was fine, but little Peter was gone. Gone to the South, where he would never ever be free. He would be a slave all his life because down there they didn't have freedom laws like they had here in New York. "What can I do," I asked some church people. "Who can I pray to, to get my little Peter back?" They sent me to some Quakers who had a place called the Quaker House. The people at the Quaker House said their business was fighting slavery and its harmful effects. They said they would take my case to the court in Kingston.

They did. And that's when I started hearin' all those educated words that I wasn't understandin'. But what I was understandin' is that they was arguin' for my right to have my son Peter back with me. They argue, and the lawyer for the Fowler family argue back. Sometime them educated people even got to shoutin' at each other in the courtroom and the judge had to bang his little wood hammer just to get them to quiet down. But in the end it turned out all right. The judge said that they had to give my Peter back to me and that was the end of it.

That was when I began to realize about the power of the law and the power of educated words to make the law work. So now I'm makin' it my business to learn all them words so I can help other people get their babies back the way I got mine. As I see it, my path is to help people like me. Women like me. But to do that it gon' take a lot of learnin'. So that's where I is right now. Startin' to learn.